A PAST and PRESENT Companion

The
GOLDEN VALLEY LINE
Swindon to Gloucester
Past and Present

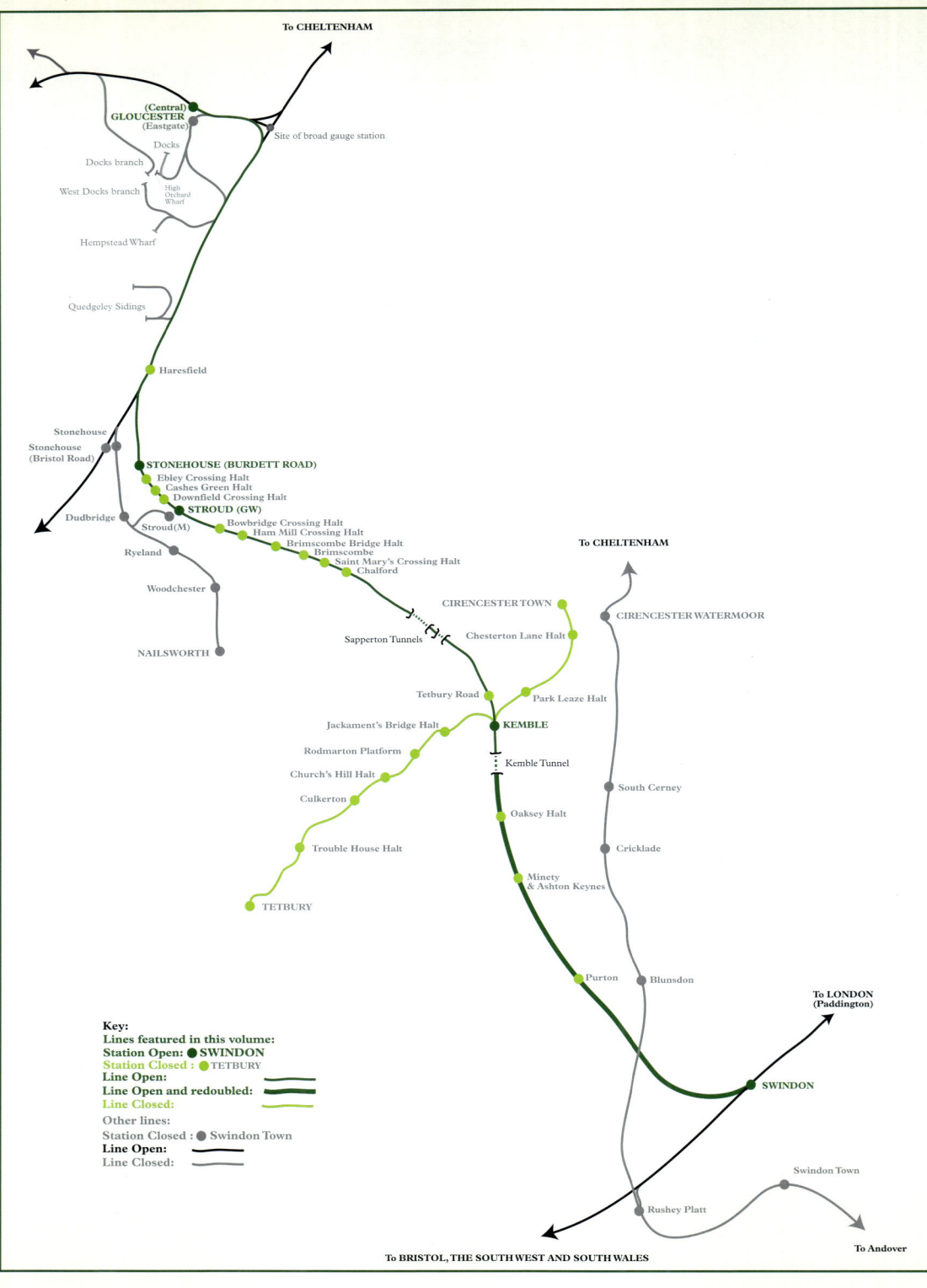

A PAST and PRESENT Companion

The GOLDEN VALLEY LINE
Swindon to Gloucester
Past and Present

John Stretton and Tim Maddocks

Past & Present Publishing Ltd

© John Stretton and Tim Maddocks 2014

All rights reserved. No part of this publication may be reproduced, stored in a retrieval system or transmitted, in any form or by any means, electronic, mechanical, photocopying, recording or otherwise, without prior permission in writing from Silver Link Publishing Ltd.

First published in 2014

British Library Cataloguing in Publication Data
A catalogue record for this book is available from the British Library.

ISBN 978-1-85895-288-8 (Softcover Edition)
      978-1-85895-289-5 (Hardcover Limited Edition)

Silver Link Publishing Ltd
The Trundle
Ringstead Road
Great Addington
Kettering
Northants NN14 4BW

Tel/Fax: 01536 330588

email: sales@nostalgiacollection.com

Website: www.nostalgiacollection.com

Printed and bound in the Czech Republic

This book is dedicated to Glyn Maddocks, 1929-2013

Acknowledgements

As always with publications delving into the past in any way, your authors are indebted to a wide variety and large number of people who have assisted in one way or another. Photographers, especially, have been very willing to submit their images for consideration and we are truly grateful to those who aided in this way – without them and their foresight in pointing the camera at strategic moments the book would have struggled to be born! They are duly credited throughout the collection, but we take this opportunity to offer all of them our profound gratitude. In addition, there are those who have helped us before and have been kind enough to put their name in the frame again!

Amongst all of these there are some who deserve special mention and we would like to offer our sincere thanks to (in no particular order): John Dagley-Morris and David Hopkins (proofreaders), Chris Baker, Garry Stroud, Commander Anne Sullivan RN, Mike Romans and various individuals from both Network Rail and FGW, who have been supportive, encouraging and accommodating. Finally, as usual, thanks go to all at Silver Link – Peter, for encouragement and for putting up with countless phone calls, and Will – for their unflinching patience and courtesy. Thank you all!
The illustrations credited 'MJS' and 'TM' are by your authors.

KEMBLE: Ex-GW 'Hall' Class loco No 5975 *Winslow Hall* plods through Kemble with an up ballast working on 28 March 1964 consisting of loaded 'Mermaid' tipper wagons. The Cirencester bay platform can be seen to the left of the train. The branch had mere days of life left at this point, finally closing on 6 April 1964. Modellers will note the 'trapping' arrangement by means of the short headshunt leading from the branch platform. *Keith Jones collection*

Contents

Foreword by Vice Admiral, Sir Tim Laurence	6
Foreword by Sir William McAlpine, 6th Baronet	7
Introduction	7
Swindon to Kemble Tunnel	9
Cirencester to Tetbury	50
Kemble to Stroud	73
Stroud to Gloucester	103
Index of locations	128

KEMBLE: On 12 August 2013 a mother and her young charges pause to get a closer look at DB Schenker's No 66138, which waits to enter the major engineering blockade that had just started between a point to the south of Kemble Tunnel and Swindon Junction. The loco was later due to haul an engineering train out of the possession on completion of its work. This was the first and main 'enabling' blockade for the redoubling project, where much of the preparatory work was done, prior to the subsequent installation of the new second track. *MJS*

JACKAMENTS BOTTOM: On 5 April 1964, on the doomed Tetbury branch, a special half-day excursion chartered by the Gloucestershire Railway Society is seen heading towards Tetbury as No 1472 propels its two auto-coaches, normally used on Chalford services, towards Kemble, close to Jackaments Bottom, with the buildings of Kemble Airfield in the background. The train left Gloucester at 2.05pm and covered both the Tetbury and Cirencester branches during the trip. *John Dagley-Morris*

Foreword by Vice Admiral, Sir Tim Laurence

BUCKINGHAM PALACE

The recently completed redoubling of the 'Golden Valley' line between Swindon and Kemble is but one example of the rejuvenation of the nation's hard pressed railway network. With the number of rail journeys now being as great as at any time since the 1920s, but on a network that is one-third of the size, it is not surprising that the need to expand the national rail system is becoming ever more pressing.

HRH The Princess Royal and I are particularly pleased that our own local line has undergone such a significant improvement, in conjunction with preparations for the forthcoming electrification of the Great Western main line between Paddington and South Wales. This will, in turn, provide the basis for further improvements to the number and quality of services on the route between Swindon and Gloucester in the future.

This volume is a fitting tribute to the planning, commitment and dedication of the various teams within the railway industry that have completed the recent transformation which is so very well captured within these pages. The words and illustrations, the sharing of 'past and present' comparisons and the images of the logistics involved all paint a vivid picture of this historic route and the improvement it has undergone.

Tim Laurence

Vice Admiral, Sir Tim Laurence

Foreword by Sir William McAlpine, 6th Baronet

I count myself extremely privileged to have been born into a family closely involved with railways. Historically, this lineage goes back to my great-grandfather, Sir Robert McAlpine, 1st Baronet (1847-1934), commonly nicknamed 'Concrete Bob' in connection with the construction of Glenfinnan Viaduct at Lochaber in the Highlands of Scotland between July 1897 and October 1898. At a cost of a little short of £19,000 for a 21-arch, single-track, parabolic-shaped viaduct, rising to some 30 metres in the crossing of Loch Shiel, it was one of the largest engineering undertakings using un-reinforced concrete, and has been one of Scotland's wonders ever since, especially in railway circles. The construction company is still in existence, and of which I have been a past director.

Born in London in 1936, I have been equally fortunate to have been around railways for most of my life and am not embarrassed to be known as a railway enthusiast. My close association came with my first job, at the company's Hayes Depot, Middlesex, which site was home to its railway locomotive and wagon fleet. Whilst there I came to know the firm's Hudswell Clarke 0-6-0ST No 31, and when, later, I learned that it was for sale at the princely sum of £100 I snapped it up and moved it to my estate home at Fawley in Buckinghamshire. From this small acorn in 1961 has grown the oak tree that is the current Fawley Hill Railway, incorporating, amongst other things, the steepest standard gauge gradient – a mile long, and 1 in 13! I am proud of this and that I have been able to add to it, amongst other things, the ex-Midland Railway signal box from Shobnall Sidings, near Burton-on-Trent, and the footbridge from Brading on the Isle of Wight's Ryde-Shanklin line.

I am also proud to have been involved with the salvation of ex-GWR 'Castle' No 4073 *Pendennis Castle* and ex-LNER 'A3' No 4472/60103 *Flying Scotsman*. I have come to love railways in their many forms over the years, but I have always had a deep affection for things Great Western, not least the geographical spread of its lines throughout the southern and western regions of the UK. The route from Swindon to Gloucester through Kemble, opened in 1845, has long had an appeal for me and I was sad to see the southern half of it singled by BR in 1968. I have long felt that the many retrenchments by British Rail were a mistake, and it is therefore gladdening to see a reversal of this trend in so many places.

The current re-doubling of the Swindon-Kemble line is to cost much more than will have been saved by that singling, but at least it will create a route that will be to 21st-century standards and will be very much needed for diversions when the main line between Paddington and Bristol/South Wales is blocked for any reason, not least during the forthcoming electrification works. The authors of this volume, celebrating the recreation, have spent many hours on and off the line in pursuit of their goal, and they have created a superb collection of pictures, encompassing not only highly evocative 'past and present' views but also glimpses of the sheer logistics of maintaining and enhancing our railways – 'men at work' that members of the public so rarely see. The result, with their trusty cameras and photographic eyes, is a wonderful record by John and Tim of what has been and what can be enjoyed in the future. They are to be congratulated and I am honoured to have been asked to write this Foreword.

Introduction

In so many areas, the value of the UK's railways is greater in sum than its constituent parts. The whole network, though spread throughout the length and breadth of England, Scotland and Wales, could, at first glance, be assessed and judged by its many parts in isolation, but the effectiveness of the whole is to a greater degree than is immediately obvious, due to routes linking one area to another. On such is the sometime-called 'Golden Valley Line' – not to be confused with the 'Golden Valley Railway' on the other side of the River Severn! – due to the descent from the summit of the line at Sapperton Tunnel to Gloucester being cut through a yellow/golden limestone ridge, between Swindon, on the Great Western main line, and Standish Junction, on the Birmingham-Bristol main line.

Opened from Gloucester Junction, immediately to the west of Swindon station, to Cirencester on 31 May

1841, under the auspices of the Cheltenham & Great Western Union Railway Act of 1836, the extension to Gloucester via Kemble (though without a station there initially) was completed on 12 May 1845. Laid to Brunel's 7ft 0¼in gauge, the line was bought by the Great Western Railway and grandly called the 'South Wales Main Line'. It was converted to standard gauge on 26 May 1872. There followed approaching a century of largely uneventful service to the nation until the Cirencester branch closed to passengers from 6 April 1964 and to freight on 4 October the following year. A branch from Kemble to Tetbury was opened on 2 December 1889 – originally planned to extend to Nailsworth – and closed to passengers on the same date as the route to Cirencester, with freight going earlier this time, on 5 August 1963.

The route covered by this volume has seen a wide variety of services, from 'main-line' trains to London to the much more humble railmotor services that ran for many years between Gloucester/Stonehouse and Chalford/Kemble. The latter ended on 2 November 1964, leaving the majority of services running from Swindon to Gloucester as locals, with occasional through trains from/to London. In steam days the line was home to the world-famous 'Cheltenham Spa Express', giving the fastest journey to London from the spa town. The whole of the 'main line' was also set to suffer from the then institutionalised 'managed decline' of the national rail network, with plans being put forward to single the entire route between Swindon and Standish Junction, leaving Kemble as the only passing place. Fortunately vociferous protests ensured the retention of the double track north of Kemble – albeit heavily rationalised and with long signal sections – but the southern 12-mile length was not so fortunate and was singled between Kemble and Swindon Loco Yard when the area was converted to Multiple Aspect Signalling in 1968. The resultant lack of operational flexibility has meant increasing timetable problems, restrictions on traffic and underutilisation of an otherwise useful piece of railway over the years as traffic volumes have continued to grow, especially since privatisation in 1994.

Recognising these strictures, together with the electrification of the London-South Wales main line on the horizon and the consequent need for a diversionary route during the necessary temporary closure of the Severn Tunnel, Network Rail began looking at the need and possibility of reinstalling a second track. Earlier plans submitted in 2008/09 were rejected by the Office of Rail Regulation, which initially decreed that the enhancement would not be included in the 2009-14 Control Period. Local MPs, authorities and many others protested and, eventually, the Coalition Government announced funding for it in the 2011 Budget. Much behind-the-scenes work led to an official launch of the project at Kemble station on 11 January 2013, following which a series of midweek night and weekend possessions and longer engineering blockades have resulted in refurbishment of the earthworks at various locations and the reappearance of a second set of steel rails alongside the existing running line. The project has also encompassed enhancements to the signalling capacity between Kemble and Standish Junction, which will increase overall line capacity and aid smoother operation of the timetable.

This volume, extending the compass to Gloucester, looks at the old days alongside comparisons with the present-day scene, as with other titles in the 'Past & Present' series, but this time also features the doubling work, in conjunction with Network Rail. Men and machines at work provide a variety of illustrations, and are mostly unseen by the general public; the whole is a fascinating exposition both of the transformation of this once sleepy byway and the logistical questions needing to be answered.

Future promise is for a much expanded level of service and even the possibility of electrification within a decade – actually proposed earlier in the late 1970s! – leading to today's 'present' views themselves becoming historic and adding interest and value to the volume you hold in your hands. Thus your authors encourage you to savour the comparisons contained herein, then travel the line in person to create your own 'Golden' memories before there is yet more change.

OAKSEY HALT: DB Schenker loco No 66124 stands at the site of the former Oaksey Halt on 12 August 2013 during the major three-week blockade between Kemble and Swindon. The loco is working train 6W77, which consists of 19 'Falcon' bogie spoil wagons. The digger in the background is loading the train with spoil from the formation of the new up line, preparatory to the laying in of new track on that alignment later in the blockade. The train arrived from Bescot via Kemble single-headed, but was due to have another loco attached to the rear, enabling the train to depart from the possession the same way it had arrived. *MJS*

Swindon to Kemble Tunnel — Section 1

SWINDON: In the first view, from 25 January 1972, we see the original entrance to Swindon station prior to its demolition. The not unattractive buildings have clearly seen better days and present a rather gloomy facade, a view clearly also held by British Rail, for whom such architectural anachronisms were not in keeping with its preferred 'white heat of technology' image.

The 'present' picture is taken from exactly the same vantage point as the earlier one, and we can see the effects of the 'white heat of technology'. A large office tower block now dominates the scene, built atop the station entrance, and for many years during the British Rail era it exuded a bland and uninspiring feel; in recent years, however, the roadway to the front of the building has been completely reconstructed, trees planted and the building cleaned, so the overall impression now is light, airy and modern. The Costa coffee outlet to the left of the entrance mirrors the growth of the 'coffee culture' in the UK today, and reflects the significant improvement in facilities now available to rail travellers from stations such as this. The Queens Hotel on the corner still survives, albeit with a slightly different name – it is now the Queens Tap. One wonders whether Her Majesty would have been amused at this change in name! *Garry Stroud/MJS*

SWINDON: The old Swindon station could perhaps have been described as being a balanced image of itself, in that almost identical platform buildings graced both the upside and downside island platforms. Here is the view on Saturday 27 March 1971 looking east, towards London, before the demolition of the entire downside buildings and platform. Although all track from the bay platforms and the south side of the island platform has already been removed, the old entrance at street level survived until after the current office block was constructed. A Class 47 locomotive and 08 diesel shunter lurk in the former sidings to the north of the upside island platform. Note the prominent gantry for the colour light signalling spanning all the through lines. For many years after the closure of the former downside island to passenger services, all trains had to use the two through platforms on the upside island, which for down trains necessitated a time-consuming crossing of running lines to access them, and the same again upon departure. A points failure in the wrong place could cause serious delays. The only facility on the down side during this time was a parcels platform, which occupied part of the downside island platform 'footprint' for many years until the early 2000s. By that time the parcels business had dwindled to nothing, and the platform stood redundant for some time, until it too was demolished to make way for a new down platform.

Returning to the same viewpoint more than 42 years later, on 3 December 2013, the office tower block is now prominent on the right of the scene, and the area occupied by rubble and an old ballast bin in the 1971 photo has now been turned into a roadway, which accesses the extensive station car park and various light industrial units behind the photographer that use converted former GWR buildings. The same signal gantry still stands at the time of writing, although Swindon Panel signal box, which controls it, is finally due to close in 2015, when control of the main lines through Swindon towards Hullavington and Corsham will pass to the new Network Rail Western Route Control Centre in Didcot. The Panel building is just visible to the lower left of the tower block, but was obscured by the former downside island building in the 1971 shot. Immediately to the left of the roadway is the new down Platform 4, which was formally opened on 21 July 2003 by Sir Richard Bowker, although services had actually started using it from the commencement of the Summer Timetable on 18 May. This was built on the site of the old parcels platform and down parcels loop, the platform fronting directly onto the down main line, meaning that down trains no longer have to lose time as they manoeuvre through the east-end and west-end crossovers, saving valuable time on timetable schedules and offering passengers more reliability and convenience. *Garry Stroud/MJS*

Swindon to Kemble Tunnel

SWINDON: In the early days of the privatised railway, on 5 June 1996, the Bristol-end bay platform at Swindon plays host to newly refurbished No 143617 forming the 1033 service from Cheltenham, which has just arrived via the Kemble route. It is clearly a warm, summery day! Note the Great Western Trains-liveried HST waiting in Platform 3, no doubt picking up some of these newly arrived passengers from the Golden Valley line.

More than 17 years later the quality of passenger accommodation appears to have increased considerably! Although it seems that South West Trains has penetrated to the very heart of FGW operations, looks can be deceiving! FGW has a very good track record of procuring 'Sprinter'-type units from various rolling stock suppliers to improve its local services, or the 'FGW (West)' service group as it is known within the rail industry. No 158888 is on hire from South West Trains to supplement the 'home fleet', enabling other FGW stock to be used elsewhere. The set stands in Platform 2 at Swindon station after arriving with 2B90, the 0920 Cheltenham Spa to Swindon local service on Monday 9 December 2013. *Both MJS*

SWINDON: The magnificent view looking west from Swindon certainly doesn't look like this any longer! On 28 June 1956 ex-GWR 'Castle' Class 4-6-0 No 5093 *Upton Castle* snakes through the facing crossover from the up main line to the up island platform with a train from Cardiff. The scene is a delight for the railway historian and modeller alike – semaphore signals and complex pointwork abound! An unidentified '94XX' pannier tank bustles along a loop line adjacent to the main lines, possibly undertaking shunting duties for the extensive locomotive works in the right background or on an inter-yard trip working. The bulk of Swindon Station West signal box looms to the left; note the brick reinforcement of its base, a wartime contingency measure. This signal box controlled the whole of the west end of Swindon station, together with the junction for the Kemble line and connections to the loco works and numerous other sidings.

The present-day scene from almost exactly the same viewpoint is very different, although the stone building in the former loco works complex with the round window to the right of the HST provides a comparative reference point. On Monday 9 December 2013 HST power car No 43093 heads 1A13, the 1030 Bristol (TM) to Paddington service, as it passes the old works and approaches Platform 3 for the Swindon stop. The site of Swindon Station West signal box and the former downside island platform is now occupied by an access road to the station car park just beyond the wire mesh fence. The former railway workshops beyond the site of the signal box still stand, albeit in private industrial use, although the roofline appears to have been changed over the years. The spire of the parish church of St Mark the Evangelist stands out above the factory roofs, hidden from view in the 1956 shot by the signal box. The church was designed by Sir Gilbert Scott and built in response to a desire on the part of the GWR to provide a place of worship and religious education for the railway workers of the new railway works and their families. The architect was subsequently responsible for the design of St Pancras station and hotel, the Foreign Office and other notable public buildings; the church was dedicated on the feast of St Mark, 25 April 1845. Swindon Works itself was closed by BREL in 1986. *Mike Timms, Milepost 92½ collection/MJS*

Swindon to Kemble Tunnel

SWINDON: On Monday morning, 26 September 1977, BR Swindon 'Cross-country' set (aka Class 120) No C509, comprising vehicles W50716, W59262 and W50675, is seen leaving the reception area sidings, fresh out of the works following overhaul and passing the depot buildings en route to Cardiff Canton via Gloucester. Swindon Works is still in full swing, undertaking overhauls of various locomotives, DMUs and other rolling stock. The Class 120 units were introduced between 1957 and 1960 and, as the name implies, were built at Swindon Works for use on cross-country services, although the old BR definition of these services does not necessarily closely correspond to the routes covered by the modern day Train Operating Company of the same name. Note the old Gresley wooden-bodied coach in blue/grey livery in the sidings, stabled next to what appears to be a Mark 1 sleeping car and a DMU vehicle.

We move forward almost 24 years to 22 June 2001 as No 43128 and set, in an earlier incarnation of FGW livery, slows for the Swindon station stop forming an up express. The train is running off the up main line onto the up relief line and will then enter one of the up platform lines. This routing was later changed when the up relief line was upgraded to provide a 70mph facing turnout at Rushey Platt, almost a mile to the west, enabling a quicker and smoother approach for up trains. The works had been closed for 15 years by the date of this photograph, and new commercial building development has already started close to the former works buildings. *Garry Stroud/MJS*

SWINDON: On an unrecorded date in 1954 'Castle' Class No 7001 *Sir James Milne* passes the vast array of sidings associated with Swindon Works on a down express, probably the down 'Cheltenham Spa Express', judging from the livery of the stock. Note the variety of wagons and other railway paraphernalia – a modeller's delight! The loco, allocated to Old Oak Common (81A) at the time, was built in 1946 and was originally named *Denbigh Castle*, but was renamed after the last General Manager of the GWR on 12 March 1948. Milne had joined the company in 1904 and started to rise through the ranks. After a brief spell in the Ministry for Transport, he rejoined the GWR in 1922, becoming General Manager from 1929 until nationalisation spelled the end of the independent company at the end of 1947. No 7001 was fitted with a double chimney in 1960 and finally withdrawn from Oxley shed (84B) in late September 1963. Appropriately enough, one of the nameplates now hangs in the GWR 'STEAM' museum in Swindon. *Keith Jones collection*

With the line to Gloucester in the background, No 1011 *County of Chester* – the last survivor of Hawksworth's 'County' Class – stands in the shed yard at Swindon on 11 October 1964, less than a month after working the 'Last County' rail tour seen later in this book at Ham Mill Halt. She was withdrawn a few weeks later on 22 November and sold to Cashmore's scrapyard at Newport, where she was sadly cut up in March 1965. Following her demise, no representatives of this most recent class of GW 4-6-0 survived the cutter's torch, but now the Great Western Society has embarked on a 'new-build' project to recreate No 1014 *County of Glamorgan*, using components from Barry scrapyard donor locomotives. *MJS*

Swindon to Kemble Tunnel

SWINDON: We take to the air now in this view of Swindon Works taken in the late 1970s or early 1980s. The mass of the huge locomotive works takes up most of the centre of the view, which is looking towards the south-east with the Gloucester line curving round from the station in the top left-hand corner towards the left-hand side of the image. Although comparatively late in the life of the works, there is still evidently a lot of work going on. Numerous items of coaching stock in 'corporate blue' or blue/grey livery can be seen, many of them seemingly DMUs. The modern-day car parks immediately to the west of the station, on the down side of the line, have already been built and the former workshops on the down side are already seeing use as industrial units. Note the neat brick wall around the limits of the works area at the bottom of the photo, effectively separating them from the adjacent residential area. Many of these dwellings would no doubt at that time still be housing railway workers and their families. The parish church of St Mark the Evangelist is just in shot in the upper right-hand corner. *Garry Stroud collection*

Swindon Works undertook some overhauls of Ivatt Class 4 2-6-0s in 1964, and here we see No 43074 from Manningham shed (55F) in August of that year. A total of 162 locomotives of this LMS design were built between 1947 and 1952, being mostly used on the London Midland Region, although a few were notably used on the ill-fated Midland & Great Northern Joint line. They sometimes attracted the rather derogatory nicknames of 'Mucky Ducks' or 'Doodlebugs', ostensibly on account of the fact that their unusual high running plates rendered them ugly in some commentators' eyes. Their design was used as the basis for the later BR Standard Class 4 2-6-0s of the 76xxx series. After receiving its overhaul, it doesn't look as if Swindon hospitality is going to extend to a full clean for 43074, although at least someone has had a go at cleaning the buffers! *MJS collection*

SWINDON: We now find ourselves in the presence of a true railway 'celebrity'. Carrying the number 3717 at this time, *City of Truro* rests in the works yard at Swindon on 17 August 1938, where she is clearly posing for an official photograph to record her in museum condition. She was built in 1903 as part of the 'City' Class of 4-4-0s, designed by G. J. Churchward, and was initially numbered 3440 until a renumbering of the class in 1912. *City of Truro* is, of course, well-known as the first steam locomotive to achieve 100mph, when running down Wellington Bank on 9 May 1904, hauling an Ocean Mails special from Plymouth to Paddington. She was eventually withdrawn from everyday service in 1931 but her special status ensured that she was preserved, initially at the new railway museum at York. In 1957 she was returned to operational condition by British Railways and was used on both normal, revenue-earning passenger services and on specials. This lasted until 1961, when she was placed on display in the GWR Museum in Swindon for another 23 years, being removed and restored to working condition again in 1984, in time for the GW 150 celebrations the following year. Over the next few years she alternated between main-line use and static museum display, but following her most recent overhaul in 2004 she has worked on a number of heritage railways, notably the Gloucestershire Warwickshire Railway and the Bodmin & Wenford Railway. She is now on display at the Shildon branch of the NRM, having been withdrawn in 2013 due to concerns about the condition of the boiler. The NRM stated that it was unlikely that the loco would be steamed again, but this is a tough old lady, so who knows what the future holds?

Prior to the opening of the 'STEAM' museum at Swindon in 2000, *City of Truro* was kept on site and is seen here in part of the former works complex with the 'Retail Outlet Village' under construction around the locomotive on 10 February 1997. She was not in running order at this time, but would be overhauled in 2004 as mentioned above. *MJS collection/MJS*

Swindon to Kemble Tunnel

SWINDON: On 8 May 1982 we see Class 40 Nos 40057 and 40084 working the return leg of the Severn Valley Railway's 'Cotswold Venturer' rail tour from York to Paddington and return. The train has just departed from Swindon and is approaching the edge of the urban area, with Barnfield Road to the right of the railway. The outward leg from York had run via Worcester, Evesham and the OWW 'Cotswold line' to Oxford and Paddington, whereas the return trip ran via Swindon, Kemble, Cheltenham and the Lickey Incline. The single line between Swindon Loco Yard and Kemble is clearly visible.

On 3 December 2013 our viewpoint is slightly further towards Kemble, but the tower block in the 1982 photo is still a prominent landmark more than 30 years later. In this view No 158887 (on hire to FGW from South West Trains) forms 2B90, the 0919 Cheltenham Spa to Swindon service. The major difference in railway terms is the fact that a second running line has now appeared, although not yet in use; the tail lights of the Class 158 give the impression of 'wrong line working', but what will become the down line is still functioning here as the single line between Swindon Loco Yard and Kemble. The road to the right of the railway has been renamed 'Galton Way' and the almost inevitable increase in general vegetation is readily apparent. Also visible in this photograph is one of the two new crossovers between the up and down lines, which were installed during the August 2013 three-week blockade to replace older crossovers located at Loco Yard, which were life-expired and of a non-standard geometry.
Garry Stroud/MJS

SWINDON: Over a long weekend immediately prior to Easter 2014, another four-day blockade of the whole route from Swindon to Standish Junction took place, to enable further track works to take place at Purton and Kemble, together with other work associated with the redoubling. On 14 April 2014 a pair of nearly new Colas Rail Class 70s – Nos 70805 (nearest the camera) and 70803 – 'top and tail' 6C43, a train of 20 auto-hoppers. The train has just finished unloading top ballast at a track slew site at Purton and is slowly approaching the end of the possession at Swindon, prior to exiting at Swindon station, reversing and returning to Westbury Yard. The train is seen here approaching signal SN157R, located at 79m 40ch, and is running on the new Up Kemble line, which at that time was not yet commissioned, the adjacent Down Kemble line still acting as the single running line until August 2014. *MJS*

This is the view looking north towards the erstwhile Bremell Sidings, from the realigned B4553 just outside Swindon on 14 April 2014. The road now crosses the railway at this point on a new overbridge. The original brick bridge is visible in the foreground, and is now used for pedestrians only, some of whom sadly clearly fancy themselves as 'graffiti artists'. A gang of contractor's staff, who appear to be well-equipped with yellow plant, are working on the new cable troughing route on the up side of the line. Buildings associated with the fuel depot are visible in the background. *MJS*

Swindon to Kemble Tunnel

BREMELL SIDINGS: In this fascinating view of the sidings on 9 May 1978, looking south, we can see the final configuration of trackwork here prior to the eventual closure of the rail connection. The main line has been singled for 10 years by this time, but the telegraph pole route still looks to be in good order. The remains of the north-end connection to the sidings can be seen in the foreground, disconnected in 1968 when the line was singled and Bremell signal box closed in connection with the Swindon area MAS project. Note the relatively tidy lineside and open feel to the scene.

The South Wales main line west of Swindon is evidently under an engineer's possession on Sunday 23 April 1978 as HST set No 253017 forms the 1250 Paddington to Swansea service, seen here in the early stages of its diversion via Kemble and Gloucester, as it passes Bremell fuel sidings. This was a wartime fuel depot, opened on 7 November 1943, and was officially listed as being 80 miles 24 chains from Paddington. Access to the sidings, which were all on the up side of the line, was controlled by a 25-lever GWR Type 13 signal box, which was opened at the same time as the sidings. In this view the signal box has long been taken out of use, having been closed on 16 June 1968 in connection with the Swindon resignalling scheme and the connection simplified to just the London end of the site. Deliveries by rail were generally superseded when a pipeline was opened in later years, although initially retained for emergency use, the connection was taken out of use in 1987 due to damage to a bridge.

Just over 35 years later the scene looks very different, as an unrecorded FGW HST set heads towards Swindon (away from the camera) on Thursday 16 May 2013, forming 1L67, the 1431 Cheltenham Spa to London Paddington service. The depot site remains but the sidings and some of the structures have long gone. Lengths of new long welded rail and stacks of new concrete troughing can be seen, already delivered to the site in preparation for the August 2013 blockade enabling the redoubling. *Tim Venton/Garry Stroud/MJS*

BREMELL SIDINGS: On 12 August 2013 the summer blockade is now in full swing. Nothing appears to have changed as regards the oil depot itself, now securely and completely fenced off from the railway that once served it, but the single line has been slewed over onto a temporary alignment, very close to the green fence. This was to facilitate the laying of the new Down Kemble line, which would take place over the next few weeks. The formation has already been prepared for this, with bottom ballast already in position, and a faint yellow alignment line can be seen, sprayed on top of the new ballast. Bremell was one of six major track renewal sites during this blockade, and work had started there at 0100hrs on 10 August, the day that the blockade as a whole commenced, continuing until 26 August. The worksite extended from 79m 60ch to 80m 50ch and was primarily to enable the single running line to be slewed. A series of spoil and ballast trains would run between Hinksey Yard (Oxford) and the blockade to supply the site, the trains being hauled by Freightliner HeavyHaul (FLHH) locomotives and worked by a variety of crews from three different Freight Operating Companies, including FLHH, DB Schenker and Colas Rail.

On 14 April 2014 No 70803 leads 6C43, an engineering train composed of 20 autohoppers from the Purton slew site, booked to exit the possession at Swindon station at 1800hrs and run from there back to Westbury Yard, via Melksham. No 70805 is marshalled at the rear, and will lead from Swindon to Westbury. The train is running on the brand new and as yet uncommissioned track of the Up Kemble line. The adjacent down line, which would remain in use under normal operational conditions as the single line between Loco Yard and Kemble until the August 2014 blockade, has also been renewed with new concrete-sleepered track. *Both MJS*

NEAR BREMELL SIDINGS: On 12 August 2013 No 66555 is seen at the London end of 6Y69, the 1250 Hinksey to Bremell worksite engineering train. it is formed of nine loaded 'Salmon' bogie wagons conveying G44 concrete sleepers for the new running line that is about to be installed on the bottom ballast to the left of the train. The train is 'top and tailed' with No 66534, which can be seen in the background, and is due to leave the possession at the Swindon end at 2359hrs that same day, for Hinksey; for this move No 66555 will be leading. The old single running line has been slewed over to the right on a temporary alignment, while a gang of track workers wait at the far end of the train for the unloading of the sleepers to commence. MJS

At the other (Kemble) end of the Bremell worksite, No 66534 – another FLHH locomotive – is seen at the opposite end of 6Y69. The slew from the former single-line alignment to the temporary situation is clear in this view. The piece of yellow plant standing next to the loco will shortly commence to unload the G44 concrete sleepers from the bogie wagons. MJS

During the August 2013 blockade Network Rail, in conjunction with main contractor Amey Colas, installed CCTV equipment to enable the project coordinators at the main site offices near Swindon to monitor progress. Here we see some telecoms contractors installing a satellite dish to connect the camera with the Project HQ. TM

NEAR BREMELL SIDINGS: Preparations are now under way to start unloading the G44 concrete sleepers from 6Y69 on 12 August 2013, with No 66534 at the far end, as ground staff employed by the FOC start to undo the straps holding the sleepers in place. Note the freshly laid 'bottom ballast' to the left of the train and the surveying equipment in the down cess. *MJS*

On 14 April 2014 train 6C43 slowly approaches the road bridge immediately to the north of Bremell, with No 70803 doing the hard work and No 70805 bringing up the rear. The train's 20 ballast autohoppers, seen earlier, are running within the confines of an engineer's possession, which extended from Standish Junction to Swindon Loco Yard for a four-day period immediately prior to Easter 2014. *MJS*

PURTON COLLINS LANE level crossing is located at 81m 09ch from Paddington. On Sunday 14 January 1973 Bristol DMU No B551 works the 1330 Swindon-Gloucester local service over the crossing. The railway has been singled at this location for almost five years, the other running line having been removed in 1968, but the level crossing configuration has been adjusted to reflect the new arrangement, with fencing extending over the old formation. At that time the level crossing was still gated but controlled by miniature red/green warning lights, somewhat unusual for a public road crossing. Prior to resignalling and singling in 1968 there was a crossing keeper here who opened the gates when safe to do so and no trains were expected, to allow any road traffic on this quiet country lane to cross the line. Note the telegraph poles and wires, still very much in use at that time and a prominent feature of the railway landscape that has now all but disappeared.

The crossing was converted to automatic half-barrier operation on 20 November 1988. With the same cottage just visible on the left-hand side, FGW HST power car No 43041 brings up the rear of 1L67, the 1420 Cheltenham Spa to London Paddington express, as it crosses the completely rebuilt Collins Lane crossing at Purton on 2 September 2014, using the new Up Kemble line. *Garry Stroud/MJS*

PURTON station was opened on 31 May 1841 and was located approximately 4 miles from Swindon, and 81 miles 36 chains from Paddington; it is seen here around 1959, looking towards Gloucester. When first built, the up platform building was constructed of wooden planks, with a small shelter provided on the down side. The former was later completely rebuilt in the late 1950s and the more modern result is seen in this photograph. The goods sidings seem to be busy and the single-road goods shed is visible in the distance; this was accessed via a loop line, which ran from both the down and up lines via trailing connections.

The locals must have considered the rebuilding of their station to be a sign of confidence in its future, but sadly this was not to be, and it was closed, together with many other local stations between Swindon and Gloucester, in November 1964. By the time this picture was taken from the same road overbridge on Sunday 26 January 1975, the scene had been almost completely transformed, with almost all railway buildings and the down platform having been swept away. Only the 1950s main station building and some remnants of the up platform survive, and the main line is now a single track – a thoroughly depressing sight!

The progress of redoubling is evident on 14 April 2014. The former single line, now on the Up Kemble formation on the right but still acting as the sole running line until the following August, has been partly renewed, as evidenced by the new ballast in the foreground, while a brand new Down Kemble line has been laid in alongside. The station building still survives, now firmly in the hands of a private garage business (the owner clearly having an interest in vintage military vehicles!), but the surrounding vegetation has grown up significantly in

the intervening 38 years. The fine orange-brick detached house clearly visible in the 1975 view can now just be seen through the trees behind the station building. *Joe Moss, Roger Carpenter collection, MJS collection/Garry Stroud/MJS*

PURTON: In this much-retouched view dating from the early 1900s, looking towards Swindon, the earlier wooden station building at Purton can clearly be seen. The road overbridge from which the previous photographs were taken also acted as the station footbridge, a pragmatic cost-saving solution, which at the time would have made a lot of sense, but which would be out of the question today, due to the much higher volumes of fast road traffic now using that road. The stationmaster and the staff pose for the picture, possibly while they wait the arrival of the next local train.

Some 70 years later the scene has been transformed, and not for the better! The station site is seen on Sunday 5 March 1972, and the remains of the station entrance from the road can still be seen in the brickwork of the overbridge, which is still adorned with the white signal-sighting patch, even though the signals here were removed in 1968 when the replacement GWR Type 7 signal box dating from 1901 was closed and the line was singled. The goods yard and various sidings were progressively removed during the early and mid-1960s. The upside goods yard seems to be still functioning as a coal yard, a not uncommon feature of many closed stations in the 1970s and 1980s. Even if the coal was now delivered and distributed by road, the coal merchant would still pay a regular rent to British Rail, which was often based on the ground area actually used for the storage of coal. One of your authors well remembers visiting the former station at Weston, near Bath, on the ex-Midland line from Bath Green Park to Mangotsfield in 1981, early in his BR career and in the company of a local BR inspector, purely for the purposes of measuring the size of the coal mounds with a measuring wheel!

The effects of 41 years are seen from a more modern angle, again looking towards Swindon on 16 May 2013. The descending post-and-wire fence on the extreme left marks the location of the erstwhile platform ramp, while the former station building, itself now more than 50 years old, is still in situ among the trees. The single line now runs approximately on the alignment of the former up line. A piece of spare rail lies in the cess, in case required for track repairs in the area, and there is little sign of the impending redoubling project, although this would soon change, with the start of the blockade now less than three months away. *Garry Stroud collection/Garry Stroud/MJS*

PURTON COMMON: During the August 2013 blockade a wagon in an engineers train became derailed between Minety and Purton Common, which unfortunately caused some track damage and required an additional worksite to be set up during the big blockade to effect repairs. The possession plan was quickly re-cast and additional materials and manpower brought onto site with commendable speed. Thanks to good work by all concerned, the repairs were completed in time for the planned hand-back of the main possession, although a temporary speed restriction was imposed for a short time thereafter to allow the track to consolidate. In this view taken at Purton Common, looking towards Swindon on 29 August 2013, we see a section of track replaced in connection with the incident.

In an earlier view from Purton Common Crossing taken on 3 December 2013, evidence of the forthcoming redoubling work is largely yet to appear, although an orange-suited track worker can be seen in the distance, possibly involved in surveying work for the project.

The shiny rails of the new Down Kemble line nearest the camera, seen on 14 April 2014, point to a high level of usage of this as yet un-commissioned piece of track by engineering trains and on-track machines, one of which is visible approximately 100 yards away. A gang of workers is visible in the distance at the site of the former Purton station. *All MJS*

Swindon to Kemble Tunnel

PURTON COMMON CROSSING: On Sunday 21 January 1973 Brush Type 4 No D1732 heads a Paddington-bound express at Purton Common level crossing, 81 miles 65 chains from Paddington. This was still controlled by a crossing keeper at this time, who would open and close the gates manually and operate the corresponding protecting signals from a small ground frame. The chimney and buildings of Hills Brickworks can be seen in the distance; these closed in 1977. Note the ex-GWR dwelling on the extreme left. The fact that the down protecting signal is cleared despite the presence of an up train may indicate that the gates are locked closed and the crossing not staffed at this time on a Sunday, the equivalent perhaps of a signal box being 'switched out'.

Some 40 years later the old signals have long gone, as the crossing is now completely unstaffed and designated as a User Worked Crossing (UWC), where anyone wishing to cross must first ring the signaller for permission to open the gates. In this view from 16 May 2013, an unidentified FGW HST set has passed over the crossing forming the 1336 service from Paddington to Cheltenham Spa. *Garry Stroud/MJS*

PURTON COMMON CROSSING: In a view full of period details to delight the modeller, we enjoy another view of Purton Common Crossing, taken on Sunday 26 January 1975, when all its original equipment and signs were still present. The gates look in reasonable condition and the ground frame hut seems to have been recently painted. The red-brick crossing keeper's house in the background is clearly of Great Western Railway origin. Again we see a heavily wired telegraph pole set against the clear winter's sky. With the exception of the TV aerial, the scene is almost timeless!

Thirty-nine years have passed, and what a contrast! Apart from the house itself, almost the only other artefact in common with the older view is the TV aerial, although even this seems to be leaning at a drunken angle now. The crossing is no longer used for vehicles, but all the modern equipment and signage for a User Worked Crossing can be seen in this view 2 July 2014, which also clearly displays the new double track. *Garry Stroud/MJS*

Swindon to Kemble Tunnel

PURTON COMMON: The view is now immediately to the north of the Purton Common crossing, in the very last week of the whole redoubling project. No 66092, still in the attractive red and gold EWS livery, stands with 6W51, the 2003 (Monday) Bescot to Purton (via Standish Junction) Balfour Beatty NTC (New Track Construction) train, in warm sunshine on Tuesday 19 August 2014. *MJS*

NORTH OF PURTON COMMON: In this view from 29 August 2013, looking towards Kemble approximately three-quarters of a mile north of the crossing seen on page 27 during the three-week blockade, further evidence of track repairs and replacement following the earlier derailment of engineer's train 6W78 can be seen. Emergency lighting has been installed to allow the repairs to continue round the clock, and a large gang of track renewals staff can be seen in the distance.

A few minutes after the previous photograph was taken one of your authors has strayed into shot, as we both walked out to the focus of that afternoon's track repairs. Some serious yellow plant can be seen in addition to the PW gang. Note that these rails have yet to have their clips added. *Both MJS*

Swindon to Kemble Tunnel

NORTH OF PURTON COMMON: On 29 August 2013, in the last days of the first blockade of the Swindon-Kemble redoubling project, two track renewal workers each operate a McCulloch Rail Trac Rail Transposer (TRT) at the track repair site approximately a mile north of Purton Common Crossing. These machines, working in tandem, cleverly and seemingly effortlessly move heavy lengths of long welded rail into the correct position on the sleepers. This is skilled work, being undertaken by qualified operators from the plant supplier.

Moments later, with the down line on the left excavated and laid with ballast ready for relaying, TRT No 16 prepares the rail for inserting into position on the new up line.
Both MJS

MINETY: On 8 September 1982 a three-car DMU (set C596) passes the site of Minety & Ashton Keynes station with an up local working, which will probably terminate at Swindon. Very little remains of the former station, which was closed to passengers on 2 November 1964, the goods yard having closed more than a year earlier in July 1963. The station was situated on the edge of the village and was previously called just 'Minety' until 1905. The new name was clearly an attempt to generate more traffic, even though the village of Ashton Keynes was some 2 miles distant.

The site is now seen on 29 August 2013, and the reader will be forgiven for failing to make any connection with the 1982 photograph, such has been the amount of tree growth and other general vegetation encroachment in the intervening years. The redoubling blockade is nearly over and Minety was one of the key track renewals sites. The new line can be seen on the right, and this will continue to act as the single running line for a few more months until the new double track is commissioned the following year, when it will become the new Up Kemble line. The older track on the left, now on the Down Kemble line formation, is in fact the original single running line, and was slewed into this position to facilitate the relaying of the up line. The older track is life-expired, and will be removed during non-disruptive overnight possessions following the end of the blockade and a new Down Kemble line laid in. The temporary lighting for the blockade track works and its associated generator can be seen next to the track. A new S&T location cabinet has been installed to the left of the down line. *John Acton, MJS collection/MJS*

MINETY: This lovely period photo shows the upside station building at Minety circa 1898, which was an original Brunel 'chalet' design. Horse-drawn transport awaits the arrival of the next up train, and all concerned appear to be aware of the presence of the photographer, judging by the attentive poses adopted. Despite having opened almost 60 years earlier in 1841, the whole scene still gives an impression of newness.

In what your authors believe to be a post-Grouping view from the late 1920s, we see Minety & Ashton Keynes station in the snow. The whole scene is clean and tidy, although the cold weather has no doubt contributed to the fact that no one appears to be about. Note the Railway Hotel through the trees on the left; this was built in 1853 and is still in business as The Vale of the White Horse Inn, a lunch venue that your authors can thoroughly recommend! *Both Chris Baker collection*

MINETY: In this undated view taken in the British Railways era, the elegant station buildings that once graced Minety & Ashton Keynes station can be seen, including the long downside waiting shelter with its overall canopy. The Brunellian 'chalet'-style main station building can also be glimpsed on the up platform. The station here was almost exactly 4 miles beyond Purton and formerly had goods loops in both the up and down direction, together with a goods yard and storage sidings on the up side. A timber goods shed was also provided. The 31-lever GWR Type 7 signal box dating from 1903 can be seen in the background, which is looking towards Kemble and Gloucester.

The former stationmaster's house can be seen behind the trees in this comparative present-day view, taken on 16 May 2013. The remains of the down platform are still extant, although it seems to have been rebuilt using breeze blocks sometime between the date of the previous photograph and closure in 1964. Redundant concrete troughing units have been neatly stacked on the old platform, waiting to be removed and recycled. The 85½ milepost can be seen to the right of the line in the distance, correctly located on the up side of the running line, as was normal practice. *Douglas Thompson, MJS collection/MJS*

MINETY: In another scene full of pleasing detail for the railway historian and modeller, ex-GW 0-6-0 pannier tank No 3763 arrives at Minety & Ashton Keynes on 31 March 1962 with the 4.18pm local train from Swindon to Kemble. Allocated new to St Phillip's Marsh in 1937, the loco was allocated to Swindon (82C) shed at the time of this photo. She was transferred to Didcot (81E) two months later, then to Old Oak Common (81A) a year later in May 1963. She was finally withdrawn from Southall shed (81C) in July 1965. The elegance of the Brunellian station buildings can be seen in this view. The up platform extended beyond the road overbridge in the background, the two platforms having been constructed to not quite lie opposite each other; there was a footbridge between them. A grey unfitted six-plank open wagon is sitting in the loading dock and there is evidence of PW work in the 'six foot' between the up and down lines.

The comparative modern-day view from 16 May 2013 shows that virtually nothing remains of the original station, although the wall of the former loading dock can be made out behind the mesh fence to the left of the single running line. *John Dagley-Morris/MJS*

OAKSEY HALT was located at 88m 35ch from Paddington and was opened on 18 February 1929 in response to local petitions for a station in the area. Situated remote from the village in the middle of the countryside, it was provided with only the most basic of facilities, as seen in this undated view. The halt was unstaffed throughout its short life, and closed at the same time as most of the other stations on the line in November 1964. No goods facilities or sidings were provided, nor was there a signal box here.

The same view on 12 August 2013, just after the commencement of the August 2013 enabling blockade, shows that all vestiges of the former station have been swept away. This was one of the first track renewal sites in the big blockade, and engineering train 6W82 with loco No 66027 at the head can be seen standing on the original single running line, temporarily slewed over to the down line formation, prior to a new up line being laid in. The 'Falcon' bogie wagons are for spoil excavated from the formation of the up line, which together with the track itself was being renewed to the regulation depth. *Richard Casserley collection, MJS collection/MJS*

Swindon to Kemble Tunnel

OAKSEY HALT: In this view taken on 16 May 2013 we can see the remains of the halt, still looking tidy after nearly 50 years of neglect, prior to the start of earthmoving and demolition of the old platforms during the August blockade. The single line stretches away into the distance towards Swindon, having been slewed almost centrally between the old platforms. Note the new long welded rail in the 'four foot', waiting for the blockade to start. Contractors have already fashioned a crude ballast crossing at the far end of the station site, probably to facilitate movement of road/rail machines on and off the track.

By 11 July the former platforms had been bulldozed away during overnight possessions in order to create sufficient room for the forthcoming track renewal works. Units Nos 153325 and 150247 pass the site forming 2G82, the 0938 Swindon to Cheltenham Spa local service. Note that the Class 153 unit, now on lease to FGW, is still in its former London Midland livery. There's no realistic possibility of passenger trains ever stopping at Oaksey again! *Both MJS*

OAKSEY HALT: On 13 August 2013 GBRf No 66717 *Good Old Boy* is at the Kemble end of 6W81, the 1005 Kemble to Bescot Up Engineer's Sidings spoil train, while tracked plant works alongside, loading spoil into the 'Falcon' bogie wagons. The new but temporary alignment of the former single line can be seen, now on the down formation. A second spoil train waits in the distance. The train is described as starting from Kemble, rather than this actual worksite at Oaksey, in order to comply with the way that train schedules are input into the TRUST train monitoring system. Crucially for train operation purposes, the engineering trains schedule does not commence inside the possession but rather at the first TRUST location on a 'live' railway. As trains were being operated from Gloucester to and from Kemble, the latter location was deemed to be the starting point for the spoil train.

Towards the end of the big blockade on 29 August, we see a road/rail machine working on the newly laid up line, which by this time has been ballasted and tamped. The original single line now occupies the down line formation, with the curved ends of steel sleepers visible. This track will not remain, however, as it was not deemed suitable for future traffic requirements, so would be relaid in due course prior to the final commissioning of the new double track in August 2014. *TM/MJS*

OAKSEY HALT: On an unrecorded date in 1964 'Hall' Class loco No 6993 *Arthog Hall* works a local train formed of three coaches and a box van from Swindon to Gloucester past Oaksey Halt. The first vehicle looks to be an ex-LMS Stanier Brake 3rd. Built in 1948, the loco was allocated to Swindon shed in 1959, then to Gloucester (Horton Road) when seen here, and was withdrawn from Oxford shed in December 1965, a mere 13 years old. Scrapping followed at Cashmore's yard, Newport, in March 1966.

Swindon to Kemble Tunnel

The second view, taken on 16 May 2013 and looking towards Swindon, is much nearer the gracefully proportioned brick and stone overbridge carrying the Oaksey to Somerford Keynes road, and the halt platforms are still in situ. This structure would make a fine scratchbuilding project for the aspiring modeller!

The third view is dated just over three months later on 29 August, as a road/rail machine works on the new Up Kemble line. The temporary, undulating nature of the slewed former single line can be seen to the right. Once the blockade finished a few days later, the new up line became the single running line and a new Down Kemble line was laid in, once the older track was removed. The new double track formation was finally commissioned on Bank Holiday Monday, 25 August 2014. *A. E. Durrant, Mike Boakes collection MJS (2)*

OAKSEY HALT: We now return to the road overbridge just north of the site of Oaksey Halt, but this time the view is looking north-west towards Kemble on 16 May 2013. The yellow milepost tells us that we are 88½ miles from Paddington.

On 14 August of that same year DB Schenker's No 66106 stands at the Swindon end of a ballast train formed of 20 bogie side-tipper wagons, which are normally formed up into semi-permanent sets of five vehicles. These are very efficient vehicles and literally do what it says on the tin – they are controlled by an operator standing on site and tip to the side, unloading ballast onto the ground. In this scene the train has brought bottom ballast to the site for the new up line formation, and approximately half the train has already been unloaded. A tracked digger is spreading the new ballast into the correct position, preparatory to another train coming to site later with track components. The last 'five set' is in the newer Network Rail yellow livery. Again, the train is standing on the former single running line, now slewed over onto a temporary alignment on the down side. A new Up Kemble line will be laid where the new ballast is going. *MJS/TM*

OAKSEY HALT: On 3 December 2013, what will eventually become the new Up Kemble line – albeit still a single line operationally – has been laid in for three months as 1L50, the 1031 Cheltenham Spa to Paddington express, approaches the site of Oaksey Halt with HST power car No 43132 leading. The new concrete sleepers for the Down Kemble line have been laid in position almost as far as the road overbridge, this work having been done after the August 2013 blockade during overnight possessions. Lengths of long welded rail sit in the 'four foot' of the single line, awaiting a future possession to be moved over into position on the down line.

More progress is evident on 2 July 2014, as power car No 43015 leads a typically clean FGW HST set at Oaksey, heading over the single line towards Swindon. The new Down Kemble line, still not yet commissioned at this time, has been laid over a series of previous midweek night and weekend possessions, but the section nearest the photographer has yet to be ballasted and tamped. Some embankment stabilisation work is evident in the foreground, next to the new running line. *Both MJS*

POOLE KEYNES: On Tuesday 13 August 2013 GBRf-liveried No 66745 *Modern Railways: The First 50 Years* is seen at the northern end of the delayed 6W84 0912 Bescot to Kemble engineer's train. No 66015 is marshalled at the Swindon end of the train, this being another example of the necessity of 'top and tail' working in many engineering possessions. The train is formed up with 'Coalfish' wagons loaded with sand nearest the camera, and some side-tipper ballast wagons at the far end, and is seen temporarily at rest at the Kemble end of the Oaksey renewals site, almost a mile from the site of the former halt. The rearmost side-tippers of the previous ballast train, 6W83, can be seen in the far distance. No 66015, which had worked 6W84 into the possession, will be 'cascaded' onto the Gloucester end of 6W83 in due course, and will then work that train out of the possession back to Bescot via Kemble, following **No 66745** and 6W84, which will depart first.

The concrete sleepers for the new Down Kemble line stretch away into the distance towards Swindon behind our intrepid photographer John Stretton, who captures the detail of modern rail fastenings for posterity. *MJS/TM*

Swindon to Kemble Tunnel

KEMBLE WICK: No 66717 *Good Old Boy*, in GBRf livery, approaches the south end of Kemble Tunnel with 6W81, the 1000hrs Kemble to Bescot train formed of 'Falcon' bogie spoil wagons on 13 August 2013. The train is approaching the detonator and lamp protection at the end of the possession, prior to exiting onto the 'live' railway and running through Kemble station and back to Bescot via Standish Junction and the Gloucester Avoiding Line.

The new Down Kemble running line is evident in the foreground at the south end of Kemble Tunnel as FGW No 150249 passes on what is still the single line with 2G85, the 1338 Swindon to Cheltenham Spa service, on 16 July 2014. The final major blockade to connect the new running line at both ends and commission the new signalling will start in little over a month from this date. *Both MJS*

KEMBLE TUNNEL: No 66138 was sent light engine from Bescot to the possession on Monday 12 August 2013 in order to haul an engineer's train out of the possession via Kemble and Standish Junction. The train concerned should have been 'top and tailed' into the job, but the northern-end loco was not available at the time of departure, hence the additional light engine movement. The section of line between Kemble station and the start of the possession is under the control of a Pilotman, due to normal signalling arrangements

having been suspended in connection with the possession works. In this view **No 66138** has exited the tunnel and has stopped to allow the Pilotman to alight (he will be returned the short distance to the station by an Amey Colas van). The handsignaller in the foreground is on duty here to pick up and replace the detonator and banner protection under the instructions of the Person In Charge Of the Possession (PICOP); he is seen with his 'Possession Limit Board' (PLB) after having obtained permission for the loco to enter the possession. Once the loco had passed this point and is clear into the blockade, the handsignaller will replace his detonators on the rail and the PLB in the 'four foot'. The red signal is SN158, located at 90m 39ch, and is being maintained at danger in order to protect the 'live' railway beyond the tunnel; it will be replaced by a new structure once the double track reaches this point, this being a classic example of how 'other uses' are found for the redundant trackbed on a previously double-track section of railway.

Turning almost 180 degrees from the earlier picture of FGW unit No 150249 on page 43, we now see the unit about to pass signal SN158 and enter Kemble Tunnel on 16 July 2014. The current extent of the new Down Kemble line is evident in this view, further progress into the tunnel being blocked by the need to keep SN158 operational until the start of the August commissioning blockade; it will then be replaced by a new three-aspect colour light signal with a route indicator and a subsidiary aspect, all designated as signal 'SW1333'.
MJS/TM

KEMBLE TUNNEL: The continuing work on the Kemble redoubling project will not see the second track installed in Kemble Tunnel until the August 2014 blockade, but preparation for its alignment is clear in this view taken on Monday 14 April. *MJS*

We now move to above the north tunnel mouth. No 66957 stands at the head of 6Y67, the 2346 (Monday) Westbury-Kemble engineer's train, ready to move forward with ballast during the work to complete the second track within and just outside the tunnel on Tuesday 19 August 2014, the first day of the final week of the Swindon-Kemble doubling project. *MJS*

KEMBLE TUNNEL: This is the view through a fly-spattered windscreen of an engineers train as it emerges from Kemble Tunnel on Tuesday 13 August 2013, conveying spoil from the Oaksey plain line renewals site during that month's enabling blockade. The route is set through the connection from the single to double line (445 points) and Ground Position Light 290 is showing a proceed aspect. The train will stop in the platform at Kemble station to drop the Pilotman off and will then proceed via Stroud and Cheltenham to it's destination at Bescot Yard.

GBRF Class 66 No. 66717 'Good Old Boy' emerges from Kemble Tunnel at the head of 6W81, the 1005 Kemble to Bescot Up Engineer's Sidings spoil train, loaded with old ballast and spoil excavated from the Oaksey plain line renewals site a few miles to the south. *TM/MJS*

Swindon to Kemble Tunnel

KEMBLE: Monday 14 April 2014 was the penultimate day of the mini-blockade prior to Easter, so the majority of the installation work on the new crossover has already been completed. The full set of points for the 'B' end of the crossover (the up main end) has already been completed, together with most of the crossover itself. The switches at the 'A' end (down main) will be installed at a later date prior to the commissioning. The PW staff in the foreground are preparing to install welded joints in the new rails. Kemble station is in the background. *MJS*

Looking in the opposite direction on the same day, a group of Colas Rail staff pause to discuss some technical aspect of the next stages in the job. The new switches of 8658B points can be seen, together with the covers from the point operating mechanisms, temporarily removed to enable installation work to continue. These new points will not be commissioned until the August blockade, so will need to be secured in the 'normal' position (i.e. for straight-on running) until then. A brand new yellow point clip can be seen lying in the 'six foot' behind the group, no doubt placed there as part of the equipment to temporarily secure these points when the railway is handed back for normal operation at 0500hrs on Wednesday 16 April. *MJS*

KEMBLE: What we've all been waiting for! Dull, overcast weather on Monday 1 September 2014 cannot hide the fact that the railway between Kemble and Swindon has not only been redoubled, but that the new works have now been commissioned. On a completely new stretch of track 1G29, the 1136 London Paddington to Cheltenham Spa service, emerges from Kemble Tunnel and approaches the station stop at Kemble. Leading power car No 43005 is passing over the 'A' end of the new facing crossover, designated 8658 points on the new controlling workstation in the Thames Valley Signalling Centre at Didcot. The 25mph speed restriction signs apply to movements through the new crossover only. Also visible is a short length of 75mph Temporary Speed Restriction on the Up Kemble line between the new crossover and the tunnel mouth, to allow the new track to consolidate. The new maximum permissible line speeds between Kemble and the new crossovers at Galton Way near Swindon became 100mph in each direction from the date of the commissioning. *MJS*

On 20 August 2013 unit No 150263 runs under the graceful stone arched bridge and into the down platform at Kemble to form 2Z29, the 1054 Kemble to Gloucester service, after moving from the up platform into the tunnel and back out again under the authority of the Pilotman. The double track towards Sapperton and Stroud stretches away into the distance, and the connection into the former Cirencester platform can be seen on the right. *MJS*

Swindon to Kemble Tunnel

KEMBLE: An ex-LMS interloper on GW territory – 'Black 5' No 44966 heads 6X58, a southbound freight formed of a long rake of box vans, on 7 February 1964, wearing a 2E shed code for Saltley, where it was allocated between April 1957 and April 1964. The curiously lower positioning of the semaphore arm on the Up Starting signal was probably due to signal sighting considerations, the station canopies obscuring a higher position.

Unit No 150263 sits in the platform on 20 August 2013 forming 2Z28, the 0955 Gloucester to Kemble shuttle. The train cannot proceed further towards Swindon due to the ongoing major redoubling blockade, which starts just outside the south portal of Kemble Tunnel. The unit has just terminated and is waiting to move forward onto the Pilotman's single line section in the tunnel before reversing back into the adjacent down platform. Despite appearances, the photograph was taken under safe, controlled conditions with the permission of the Pilotman, who was not present, having been previously conveyed by road to the south end of Kemble Tunnel to accompany an engineer's train out of the blockade. Note how the vegetation on either side of the operational platforms has grown in the intervening years, although the whole scene presents a cheerful and well-kept aspect. *MJS collection/MJS*

Cirencester Town to Tetbury

Section 2

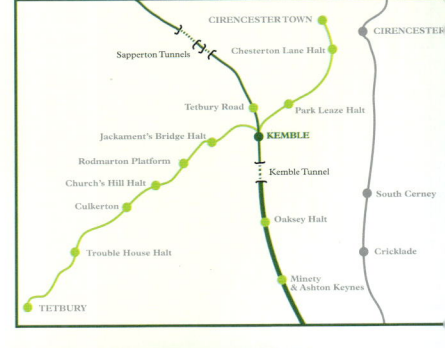

CIRENCESTER: In this 1961 aerial view of Cirencester Town station and goods yard, the full extent of the railway facilities once provided for this Cotswolds town can be seen. The passenger station is in the top right of the picture, with a pannier tank shunting a rake of goods wagons in the sidings opposite the platform. The layout is fully signalled, with the signal box visible in the centre of the view. The immediate environs of the station appear rather rural in nature. The branch line to Cirencester Town was originally part of the Cheltenham & Great Western Union Railway, which opened in 1841 from Swindon to Kemble and Cirencester. The line was subsequently extended from Kemble to Standish Junction on the Bristol to Gloucester line four years later, which resulted in the 4½ miles from Kemble to Cirencester becoming a branch line, by which time the GWR was in charge, having absorbed the C&GWUR in 1844.
Cassandra Murdoch collection, MJS collection

CIRENCESTER: Information for potential car park users is clearly laid out on chalk boards at the front of Cirencester Town station, as one of the AC Cars railbuses waits in the platform for custom in 1961. These compact units had been introduced on both the Cirencester and Tetbury branches in February 1959, in an attempt to cut operational costs and boost patronage, and were apparently quite successful, causing comment in the local communities they served. One junior school at least is reported to have taken its pupils for a return trip on the new railbus and given them a little project to do about their trip on their return to school! The Brunellian station building at Cirencester Town was given a modernising facelift to coincide with the introduction of the new railbuses, but in the end it was sadly all in vain.

On a dull 25 August 2013 the same view shows the extent of changes wrought over the years. The former Cirencester Town station is now a car park, although a short section of the original platform remains in situ, to the left of the small white car. The canopies have gone, but the distinctive Cotswold stone wall to the right of the scene remains. *D. Chandler collection, MJS collection/MJS*

CIRENCESTER: The full extent of the station buildings and canopy are revealed in this shot of the Town station on 31 March 1964, just a few days before final closure. Even by this late stage a complex of trackwork and signalling equipment remains in situ. An unidentified AC Cars railbus sets off as the 10.40am service to Kemble. Five of these machines were built in 1958, and the first was allocated to the Scottish Region, remaining there throughout its life, but Nos W79975-78 were all allocated to Swindon. Here they received a number of modifications, including retractable steps to enable them to call at the low wooden platforms of the new halts opened in connection with their introduction. Three diagrams were operated in order to maintain the timetabled service, which normally left one unit spare on shed at Swindon to cover failures or maintenance requirements. After the closure of the two branch lines in April 1964, the four railbuses were transferred to Yeovil (two units for the shuttle to Yeovil Junction) and Bodmin, where the remaining two units were used on the Bodmin North to Boscarne Junction shuttle service. When even these lines closed, the units were transferred to join the original example in Scotland. Following final withdrawal, three of the five were preserved.

In the second, post-closure, view from the mid-1960s, the station itself looks more or less intact, and almost fit to receive passengers, but the weed-grown trackbed tells its own story, and no trains are ever likely to return here again.

The intervening years have seen the whole scene tidied up and many of the station buildings removed, although the original Brunel-era structure remains. Tarmac and white lines now rule in the area where trains once ran, but at least the site is still serving a useful function for the local community, even if not one that most railway enthusiasts would prefer to see!

John Dagley-Morris/D. Chandler, MJS collection/MJS

Cirencester Town to Tetbury

CIRENCESTER: Prior to the introduction of the diesel railcars, No 5509 sits at the head of its two-coach train to Kemble on an unrecorded date in the 1950s. The loco was shedded at Swindon (82C) at the time, although it would finally be withdrawn from Truro on 30 December 1961. There is much of interest to the modeller in this view, from the detail on the locomotive to the point rodding and PW equipment in the foreground. Note the interesting configuration of the trap points in the run-round loop and the adjacent siding. It also looks as if someone in the station building now has the capability of watching TV.

The view towards the buffer stops on a decidedly damp but unspecified date in the early 1960s sees one of the AC Cars railbuses waiting on the stop blocks for custom. Again, there is more detail in this view to help any modellers of this era. One wonders how much more use the loading gauge to the left of the railbus will now see. Since the closure of the branch line from Kemble, Cirencester has become one of the largest settlements in the region without its own rail station. *John Dagley-Morris/Cassandra Murdoch collection, MJS collection*

CIRENCESTER: In a delightful scene, captured on 31 March 1964, the AC Cars railbus seen on page 52 leaves the station as the 10.40am service to Kemble, passing both the signal box and pannier tank No 1658 engaged on shunting the morning goods to Kemble. The old locomotive shed can be seen in the background, behind the GWR Type 5 signal box. An allotment for railway staff is in the right foreground, possibly used by the signalman, who can be seen returning to the warmth of his box after delivering the single-line token for Kemble to the driver of the railbus.

In a photograph taken of necessity a little further back towards the site of the station, this is the present-day view of Cirencester Town goods yard, facing south on 25 August 2013. The inevitable supermarket and a new road now block the way beyond the Cotswold dry-stone wall, built across where the spread of tracks used to be. *John Dagley-Morris/MJS*

Cirencester Town to Tetbury

CHESTERTON LANE HALT was opened on 2 February 1959 in connection with the introduction of the new railbus services. Facilities were pretty basic – almost non-existent, one might argue. In this view taken on 14 May 1959, unit No W79975 is about to depart as the 10.50am Cirencester Town to Kemble service. Note the oil tail lamp on the rear of the unit and the separate pedestrian footbridge. After being transferred to Scotland when the Yeovil Junction shuttle was withdrawn, this unit went on to work between Ayr and Kilmarnock together with the three other AC Cars units, replacing similar Park Royal railbuses, which had been giving mechanical problems. New in August 1958, No W79975 was withdrawn in December 1967 and scrapped by T. W. Ward at Inverkeithing the following August, after less than 10 years in service. *John Dagley-Morris*

On 5 April 1964 the well-documented Gloucestershire Railway Society farewell special headed by No 1472 passes under the Cirencester to Somerford Keynes road. The headboard has evidently been removed, apparently at the request of the photographer! *MJS collection*

PARK LEAZE HALT was the second very small wooden halt to be provided on the Cirencester branch in connection with the new railbus services, opening on 4 January 1960, less than a year after Chesterton Lane. In this view taken on 31 March 1964, we find ourselves between the Somerford Keynes road bridge and Park Leaze Halt looking west, as one of the AC Cars railbuses passes forming the 11.00am Kemble-Cirencester Town service.

It's hard to imagine a sharper contrast in this view of the erstwhile trackbed between Park Leaze and Cirencester taken on 25 August 2013, looking towards Cirencester. It seems pretty clear that trains are unlikely ever to run through here again. *John Dagley-Morris/MJS*

KEMBLE: In this pleasant period view dating from 1951, we see the upside frontage at Kemble station, welcoming the prospective traveller. Despite being signed as a 'car park' in the right-hand corner, the only wheeled vehicles to be seen are a collection of bicycles! The main lines and the Tetbury bay are over to the right of the main building, with the Cirencester branch platform to the left of the picture.

In the present-day view, taken on 25 August 2013, we can see that the building itself has scarcely changed over the years; if anything, the warm Cotswold stone façade has been cleaned at some stage. The building has been modified at the extreme left-hand end, where the Cirencester bay platform used to be. Modern road transport is now in evidence, although less than one would see on an ordinary day, because this view was taken during the redoubling blockade, when all trains terminated at Kemble from Gloucester, with rail replacement buses taking the passengers onwards to Swindon. *Joe Moss, Roger Carpenter collection/MJS*

KEMBLE: Churchward 'Small Prairie' No 4542, in very clean unlined BR black livery, waits in the Cirencester branch platform on an unrecorded date in 1956 with the next branch train, as No 7794 brings in a goods train from Cirencester, which appears to include two passenger coaches. No 4542 is recorded as having been shedded at Newton Abbot for the whole of its BR life, so perhaps it was on a running-in turn from Swindon Works on this occasion.

The scene changes by 1959, as No W79978 waits to depart for Cirencester Town on the morning of 22 October. This railbus was delivered new from AC Cars in November 1958, was withdrawn from the Scottish Region in February 1968, and is now preserved at the Colne Valley Railway. We don't recognise the briefcase on the platform as being official British Transport Commission issue, so perhaps it belongs to the photographer?

In comparison with the earlier historical views of the Cirencester branch platform, the contemporary view taken on 16 May 2013 is distinctly underwhelming as regards interesting period details! At least the former platform survives as a siding, which normally sees regular usage as a convenient location to stable tampers and other 'on-track' machines between Swindon and Gloucester. Trees have now grown up along the former railway boundary in the middle distance and the trackbed of the former branch line is now a well-used car park for approximately 200 yards beyond the buffer stop. *Joe Moss, Roger Carpenter collection/R. B. Parr, MJS collection/ MJS*

Cirencester Town to Tetbury

KEMBLE: '8750' Class 0-6-0 pannier tank No 3739 is coupled to a two-coach branch set comprising vehicles Nos W6447 and W6448 on an unrecorded date in the late 1950s. The loco has the early British Railways 'cycling lion' crest on the tank sides and certainly looks clean enough to have recently come out of Swindon Works, but she was actually shedded at Swindon (82C) between May 1953 and February 1963. Sadly her pristine condition in this view was not enough to prevent her from being scrapped at Cashmore's, Newport, in March 1965.

Another '8750' pannier tank, this time No 9602, waits with a Cirencester branch train at Kemble on 6 April 1957. This service must have been a goldmine to local spotters, as this is yet another 'foreign' loco on a running-in turn from Swindon Works – No 9602 was allocated to Fishguard & Goodwick shed (87J) at the time. A member of the station staff assists a lone passenger onto the train. Another set of coaches sits in the loop, no doubt having worked an earlier train on a different coaching stock diagram.

The view on 16 May 2013 shows the area of land next to the branch platform that was formerly occupied by the running loops in the earlier black and white views. Part of this area has become a 'stone bin', recently constructed by Network Rail PW staff to support the operation of stoneblowers in the area. These clever pieces of equipment automatically blow stones of a smaller grade than standard ballast underneath sleepers to adjust the level of the track to the correct height. Many of these standard-design stone bins had been constructed all over the Western Route of Network Rail at this time. *John Dagley-Morris/Mike Timms, Milepost 92½ collection/MJS*

KEMBLE: The up starting signal has been cleared for ex-GWR 4-6-0 No 1011 *County of Chester*, which is seen leaving Kemble with a Gloucester to Swindon semi-fast service on 17 August 1956. Permanent way work appears to be in progress in the 'six foot' between the up and down lines. An '8750' pannier tank, on the right, looks to be in the process of running round a three-coach branch set in the Cirencester platform.

The overall scene is much simplified some 25 years later, as three-car 'Metro-Cam' unit No B813 departs from Kemble for Swindon on 2 November 1981. The remains of the Cirencester bay can just be glimpsed through the fencing adjacent to the DMU, and the down platform on the left has at least been resurfaced with tarmac at some stage in the intervening years. The signal controlling access to the single line ahead of the DMU is just out of shot to the right.

We fast-forward a further 25 years now to see **No 43132** leading **1L72**, the 1545 Gloucester to Paddington service, on 19 September 2006, wearing the earlier version of the FGW livery. A stoneblower sits in the former Cirencester branch platform next to a very full stone bin. The platforms have acquired a yellow warning line and there is now more vegetation. The late afternoon sunlight gives a particularly cheery feel to the scene on this late summer's day. *Mike Timms, 92½ collection/ John Acton, MJS collection/MJS*

KEMBLE: On an unrecorded date in the early/mid-1960s, No D1063 *Western Monitor*, in maroon livery with small yellow panels, works a Cheltenham-Paddington express. Introduced into traffic in May 1963, the loco would be repainted into BR 'corporate blue' with full yellow ends on 11 October 1968 and would carry this livery until final withdrawal in April 1976, after notching up 1,184,000 miles in service. The photograph may well have been taken between the introduction of this loco in 1963 and its transfer to Swansea (Landore) depot in June 1964.

Leaving Kemble station and heading towards the single-line section on Friday 11 January 2013, No 43047 restarts the 1031 Cheltenham Spa-Paddington HST shortly before the start of the official launch event for the Swindon-Kemble Redoubling Project at Kemble station that same day. A ground frame has appeared next to the headshunt of the former Cirencester branch platform, this being the method of control for these points following the closure of Kemble signal box in 1968. *Garry Stroud collection/MJS*

KEMBLE: Two of the most attractive Modernisation Plan diesels feature in this view of Kemble taken on 4 April 1964, just two days before the closure of both the Cirencester and Tetbury branches. 'Hymek' No D7050 arrives in the down platform working 2B79, the 4.25pm service from Swindon, as an unidentified 'Western' in maroon livery powers up to depart with the 3.50pm Cheltenham (St James)-Paddington express. One of the AC Cars railbuses waits with a connecting service to Cirencester Town. Followers of PW practice will note the track in the siding on the extreme right, which features concrete 'pot' sleepers and steel tie-bars to hold the track in gauge.

In the second view, without trains, taken on 19 September 1983 we can see the effects of the removal of most of the signalling equipment, although the set of points to the former Cirencester run-round loop has yet to be removed and replaced by plain line. The water tower is still extant behind the downside station buildings, but the tall header tank that was mounted on top and visible in the 1964 photograph has now been removed. *John Dagley-Morris/MJS collection*

Cirencester Town to Tetbury

KEMBLE: Prior to the introduction of the railbuses, Non-auto-fitted '58XX' 0-4-2T locos were used on some of the Kemble to Tetbury branch services. The doyen of the class, No 5800, is seen here in the late 1950s running round the stock of the Tetbury branch train some time prior to the loco's withdrawal from Swindon shed (82C) on 12 July 1958. Note the six fire buckets at the end of the station building, standing by to deal with any eventuality, and the curious wooden platform extension to the right of the railwayman striding purposefully towards the coaches. One wonders what the two wicker hampers on the platform might contain – have they come from Tetbury or are they destined for that town? The photographer's brother looks quizzically at the camera.

Turning through 180 degrees, we can now enjoy a view from 1951 towards the north-west, with the Tetbury branch curving away to the left and the main line towards Chalford and Stroud to the right. The wooden platform extension can be seen much more clearly, as can two attractive ex-GWR bracket signals. The building shaped somewhat like a locomotive shed in the background is actually a steam-powered water pumping station, installed in December 1903; it was located close to a well, which was originally used to supply Swindon Works with water, the local supply apparently having an excessively high salt content. The Kemble water was initially pumped by a horse-worked device and transported to Swindon by rail in tank wagons, but as the need for water in the works grew it was decided to install a pipeline and a pumping station to supply it. The water was initially pumped into the main, large water tank at the Gloucester end of the down platform, while the higher, smaller tank was used to supply the local village area. In 1935 electric pumps took over the main pumping duties from the original steam pumps, although the latter were retained for some years on a standby basis, such was the importance of this water supply.

John Dagley-Morris/Joe Moss, Roger Carpenter collection, MJS collection

KEMBLE: The unconventionally located bracket bay platform starting signal has been lowered at Kemble for one of the AC Cars railbuses to depart as the 5.00pm service to Tetbury on 4 April 1964, in the final days of passenger services. Departure cannot be that imminent, however, as the Guard hasn't yet removed the tail lamp from this end of the railbus and placed it at the opposite end. The pre-cast concrete post is somewhat rare in GW signalling practice, as is the location of the bracket signal, presumably for reasons of space. The siding beyond the run-round loop is busy with goods wagons, and there is even a box van in the platform behind the railbus. It almost looks as if it could become 'tail traffic' for the railbus, but this was not permitted with any of the railbuses, even those built by Waggon & Maschinenbau, which actually had proper buffers, and certainly not with the AC Cars examples.

The corner of the stone building on the down platform can be seen peeping above the ubiquitous shrubbery in this view of the erstwhile Tetbury platform at Kemble on 25 August 2013 – it was hidden by the railbus in the previous view. The trackbed of the former platform and run-round loop lines has now become a rough access road, to enable vehicles to get to a compound and road/rail machine access point just to the north of the station. It is otherwise hard to imagine the former scene when standing there today, although other remnants of the Tetbury bay platform can be found concealed in the undergrowth. *John Dagley-Morris/MJS*

Cirencester Town to Tetbury

RODMARTON PLATFORM is seen in this classic view from the adjacent main road, with much to interest the modeller, as an AC Cars railbus pauses on 4 April 1964 forming the 3.45pm service from Kemble to Tetbury. As can be seen by its conventional-length platform, this halt pre-dated the introduction of the railbus services by several decades, having been opened in September 1904. Following the closure of the temporary wartime halt at Jackaments Bridge in 1948, Rodmarton was the first station upon leaving Kemble, and was also reputedly the first such station on the GWR to be accorded the status of 'Platform', although it was unfortunately some distance from the village it served.

As with so many comparative views, it is perhaps difficult to reconcile this view of the site of the erstwhile Rodmarton Platform as seen from the A433 Cirencester-Tetbury road on 25 August 2013 with that taken back in 1964, yet the dry-stone walls and general 'lie of the land' confirm that this is indeed the same place. Tree growth has replaced railway infrastructure along the embankment, to such an extent that it is impossible to see from this angle whether the old steel girder bridge remains in place or not! *John Dagley-Morris/MJS*

CHURCH'S HILL HALT: Now here is what one might describe as the 'basic railway!' This is Church's Hill Halt, the next 'station' beyond Rodmarton Platform, seen on an unrecorded date in the early 1960s, looking towards Kemble. This most basic of facilities was opened in 1959 in connection with the introduction of the railbus service. Clearly passengers were not encouraged to linger here, although at least a nameboard has been provided – perhaps one should be grateful for small mercies! PW 'aficionados' may like to note the concrete-sleepered bullhead track and the relative paucity of ballast.

In common with Rodmarton Platform, the present-day view of the site is now located in what appears to be woodland. This is the view looking towards Kemble on 25 August 2013. Nothing remains of the former halt and it is perhaps difficult enough to recognise that a railway once ran along here. *MJS collection/MJS*

Cirencester Town to Tetbury

CULKERTON was originally the only intermediate station on the branch when it opened, but was closed to passenger traffic on 5 March 1956, due to falling receipts and, allegedly, the poor condition of the platform, although it remained open for goods traffic. Its plight was actually debated in Parliament on 14 June 1956, when Anthony Kershaw, the MP for Stroud, raised concerns in the House of Commons and debated the closure with Hugh Molson, a junior minister in the Ministry of Transport, who stated that passenger receipts latterly amounted to no more than £30 per year and that the repairs to the platform would cost some £300! The junior minister appeared relatively unmoved, although the station would eventually reopen in 1959 with the introduction of the railbus services. Its rather ramshackle nature is evident in this photograph, and the £300-worth of repairs allegedly required to the platform does not seem to have been expended yet, as an AC Cars railbus calls at the reopened station on an unrecorded date in 1964. The station is now unstaffed and looks completely moribund. Note the proximity of the main road on the right and the gate on the left for the footpath entrance from the adjacent lane.

Yes, this used to be Culkerton station! The present-day view looking towards Tetbury was taken on 25 August 2013 and, unlike some of the other 'woodland scenes' we've seen, appears to be well cared for as part of someone's private garden. The former pedestrian entrance from the lane can just be seen through the trees on the left. *Mike Boakes collection/ MJS, with permission*

CULKERTON: In 1951 'Prairie' tank No 4550 is seen departing from Culkerton station with a mixed train from Tetbury to Kemble. The goods shed still retains its GWR-era paint colours of light and dark stone, and is unlikely to have received a repaint prior to closure to goods in August 1963. Its large size reflected the early hopes of the GWR that the station would attract a significant amount of both passenger and goods traffic from the surrounding district, being situated approximately halfway between Kemble and Tetbury. Sadly this was not to be, and even by the comparatively early date of 1951 the whole scene was beginning to look run down and neglected.

The modern-day view was taken on 25 August 2013 and is from a slightly different angle from the 1951 shot, being somewhat to the right, as the original view is now shielded by tree growth, making a comparative view difficult. The goods shed is boarded up but appears to be in reasonable condition. The white house in the background was the old stationmaster's dwelling. On the date of the photo, this building was for sale, apparently with planning permission granted for demolition!

Finally, the old goods shed is seen from other end, i.e. nearer the former stationmaster's house, on the same day. The former running lines ran to the right of the building, where the seemingly impenetrable hedge now stands. *Joe Moss, Roger Carpenter collection, MJS collection/MJS (2)*

Cirencester Town to Tetbury

TETBURY: In a delightful period view of a country branch line goods train, BR (WR) pannier tank **No 1664** shunts a rake of BR-built 16-ton mineral wagons in the yard at Tetbury on 9 July 1963; they had probably conveyed house coal for coal merchants at the town. The large brick goods shed looms in the background. Like virtually all its class mates, No 1664 had a scandalously short working life, having been introduced into traffic in March 1955 allocated to St Blazey shed, moving from there to Swindon shed in December 1961. She was withdrawn from Swindon in November 1964, after little more than nine years in service.

On 25 August 2013 the area formerly occupied by the pannier tank and the adjacent tracks is now grassed over, but fortunately the old goods shed has survived the passage of time, and now part of the building is in use as a local museum. The former cattle dock, hidden from view by No 1664 in the 1963 view, can be seen here through the trees, another survivor from a bygone age. *Mike Boakes collection/MJS*

TETBURY: What appears to be a pannier tank, running bunker-first with two coaches, forms a return service from Tetbury to Kemble on 27 April 1955. The branch engine shed can be seen on the left, a sub-shed of 85B Gloucester (Horton Road). Modellers will recall that this typical GW branch line shed formed the subject of a 4mm scale card kit by 'Prototype Models' in the 1970s, and will thus have graced many model layouts of Great Western branch termini. Once steam had been replaced by the diesel units, the shed continued to see use, housing an AC Cars railbus overnight.

This is the present-day view of the approach to Tetbury station past the site of the old engine shed on 25 August 2013. The route of the track is marked with occasional sleepers, but the shed now lives on only in photographs and hopefully in model form on numerous layouts! *Richard Casserley, MJS collection/MJS*

TETBURY: On an unrecorded date in the early 1950s a very presentable No 1648 departs from Tetbury with a local service to Kemble, formed by auto-coach No W59W, passing the loco shed and rather rickety-looking coaling stage. The loco was not auto-fitted, so would have to run round at the end of each journey. No 1648 was completed in May 1951 and allocated initially to Swindon shed (82C), transferring subsequently to South Wales and being withdrawn on 31 May 1963 from Neyland shed, after a short working life of only 12 years. She was cut up at Cashmore's yard, Newport, later in 1963. These were useful little locomotives, being the most modern of the traditional GWR pannier design to be built in any numbers. Their light weight of 41t 12cwt gave them a usefully wide route availability. They would have been ideal for many of the shorter preserved lines today, but sadly only one example of the class – No 1638 – has been preserved, and can now been seen in use on the Kent & East Sussex Railway. *MJS collection*

Our photographer has captured a wealth of interesting detail for modellers in this view of the doyen of the non-auto-fitted '58XX' Class of 0-4-2Ts, No 5800, at Tetbury with a train to Kemble on 6 April 1957. The station is largely intact and the platform has not yet been shortened. Note the rather 'grotty' track in the platform road – no pristine ballast here! The run-round loop also seems to have a shortage of ballast (or 'grot') between the sleepers, and there is a non-standard block-built storage hut adjacent to it – a very real artefact of the railway of that era, but not something that you see modelled very often. The crew seem to be aware of the photographer and have probably been asked to pose for posterity. Another photographer lurks behind the stout fence post on the right. *Mike Timms, Milepost 92½ collection*

TETBURY: Here we see another view of No 1472 and the 'Last Steam Train' half-day excursion that was run from Gloucester on the final day before closure on 5 April 1964. The loco was allocated to Gloucester (Horton Road) (85B) and would have been mostly used on the Chalford auto-trains at that time. She was withdrawn a mere seven months after the date of this photograph. By this time, the branch service had been in the hands of the AC Cars railbuses for some five years and the results of the shortening of the platform can clearly be seen, technically removing passenger access to the station's lavatorial facilities!

It's hard to believe that this really is the same place, and that all the structures of Tetbury station stood on this spot. Almost 50 years have passed, more than enough time for mature-looking trees to have established themselves. On 25 August 2013 a selection of old sleepers mark the curve of the platform line and run-round loop, although their spacing is a little too regular for your authors to believe that they are actual survivors from the demolition of the branch in the 1960s. Still, they nevertheless enhance the scene and act as a visible reminder of the original purpose of this site. A bench completes the scene for those who wish to pause and reflect on times past. *John Dagley-Morris/MJS*

Kemble to Stroud — Section 3

KEMBLE: On 31 March 1962 No 7035 *Ogmore Castle* roars into Kemble station with the up 'Cheltenham Spa Express'. Note the concrete GWR Type 9 signal box dating from 1929, which had replaced two earlier signal boxes at this location, Kemble West and Kemble Junction East. Some of the semaphore signals controlled from here can be seen, and a loading gauge stands guard on the right over a small siding, should anyone have the temerity to attempt to despatch an 'out of gauge' load onto the main line without the proper authority. Kemble has always only ever served a small village directly, and still does to this day, but remains open and very busy because of the wider area that it also serves. The original station was opened in May 1841, but the local landowner, one Squire Gordon, decreed that passengers could not join trains there, so the original wooden-platformed station was used purely for the purposes of changing trains. Locals had to use a separate station known as Tetbury Road, about a mile towards Stroud. This had opened in 1845 and continued to be the local station for the village until after Squire Gordon's death, when his heir, Miss Anna Gordon, agreed that a proper station could be built at the junction. This was built from Cotswold stone and opened in 1882 in a neo-Tudor style, and most of the original buildings survive in excellent condition to this day.

In a view taken slightly further back towards Swindon on 12 August 2013, DB Schenker No 66138 arrives at Kemble with 0W78, a light engine working from Bescot Yard. It will enter the main blockade just the other side of Kemble Tunnel, and haul an engineering train out of the possession and back to Bescot. The former signal box is, of course, long gone, but the old water tank survives. The double track to Stroud and Gloucester curves away into the distance, and it is worth reminding ourselves that the original British Rail 'master plan' had been to single the entire line between Swindon and Stonehouse. Fortunately protests led to the curtailment of the project once the line had been singled between Swindon and Kemble, leaving the remainder of the route northwards to Standish Junction as double track. *Cassandra Murdoch, MJS collection/MJS*

KEMBLE: The water tower and its two tanks are seen in all their glory in 1951, with the Tetbury branch curving away to the left. Note the profusion of telegraph poles and wires.

The latticework of the former supports for the higher water tank is mirrored by the modern-day mobile phone masts that stand ahead of No 150233 as it leaves Kemble on 13 August 2013 forming 2Z27, the 0952 Kemble to Gloucester shuttle, during the big redoubling blockade. *Joe Moss, Roger Carpenter collection, MJS collection/MJS*

Kemble to Stroud

KEMBLE: An unusual sight at Kemble on 26 August 1959 as No 5000 *Launceston Castle* and No 7000 *Viscount Portal* double-head the 2.15pm Paddington-Cheltenham Spa express. Why this train is double-headed is not recorded, but it may have been a way of working one of the locos to Gloucester. No 5000 was allocated to Swindon shed at the time, but No 7000 was allocated to Newton Abbot, so what it was doing on this train is something of a mystery! Modellers may wish to note the profusion of GWR round-section point rodding in the foreground. *The late Richard Dagley-Morris, John Dagley-Morris collection*

One of the former Western Region running-in boards for Kemble is now in private hands. The owner said, 'I bought this sign at the Worcester MPD Open Day on 12 April 1969 for half a crown (2s 6d). The totems were five bob (5 shillings), as they were smaller and more in demand! I then balanced it on my bicycle and wheeled it home up the very steep London Road (we lived in Worcester at the time).'

The Golden Valley Line Past and Present

SAPPERTON SIDINGS: On a crisp winter's day, 7 January 2001, DG/UK-liveried tamper No DR 73805 is on tamping duties on the Up Kemble line to the south of Sapperton Tunnel. No 66063 in the then livery of EWS Railways can be seen on the left, marshalled at the rear of an engineering train during a weekend possession. DG/UK as an organisation would subsequently become Colas Rail. *MJS*

A little closer to Sapperton Tunnel on the same day, we see a road-rail machine standing on the Up Kemble line, lifting a length of redundant rail clear of the running lines. The engineering train with No 66063 appears to have moved further on towards the tunnel. Since this date 'full orange', including trousers, has become mandatory for all Network Rail and contractor personnel working on or about the line. *MJS*

SAPPERTON SIDINGS: The relative complexity of the steam-era layout is still intact in this view of Sapperton (94m 32ch from Paddington), looking towards Swindon on 29 July 1970. Up and down goods loops are provided, together with a down refuge siding on the right hand side, albeit that by this date the rails appear rusty with disuse. Banking engines that had been attached to up freight trains at Brimscombe were usually detached here and sent back down the bank to await their next duty. The GWR Type 7B signal box was provided in 1900, although a new 27-lever frame was installed in 1941. An adjacent signal box at Sapperton Tunnel had closed in 1901, with all control of the area vested in Sapperton Sidings box. The signal box itself did not have long to go by the time this photo was taken, closing on 5 October that year, together with the surviving boxes between here and Standish Junction, as Gloucester Panel extended its area of control. The operational boundary between the Thames Valley Signalling Centre (successor to Swindon Panel) and Gloucester Panel remains at 94m 70ch to this day (actually between the two Sapperton Tunnels).

The view from the same private road overbridge on 19 August 2013 is very different, as No 150263 passes the site of the former signal box and down refuge siding with 2Z31, the 1152 shuttle service from Kemble to Gloucester. Note the new signal (bagged over) to the left of the 'Sprinter' unit; it is designated UK94 ('UK' standing for 'Up Kemble'), and is one of a number of new signals installed on both lines as part of the redoubling project, to increase line capacity between Swindon and Standish Junction, enabling a full diversionary HST service to operate between London and South Wales during GW Main Line electrification, together with the timetabled local services. *Will Adams/MJS*

SAPPERTON TUNNEL: Looking in the opposite direction from the same bridge on 5 April 1964, we see the south portal of Sapperton Short Tunnel, and No 1472 working the Gloucestershire Railway Society 'last day' special for the Tetbury and Cirencester branches. The '14XX' is now propelling its two auto-coaches back towards Gloucester, although judging by the fact that the down starting signal is still 'on', the train seems to be waiting for the signalman to obtain 'Line Clear' from Frampton Crossing box ahead. Note the two sidings in the 'quarry' area, which appear little used, and the up home signals for Sapperton Sidings signal box; the smaller 'doll' controls the entrance to the up goods loop. Also notable is the general lack of vegetation in this scene, even for 1964!

On 19 August 2013 we see No 150263 again, working 2Z31, the 1152 service from Kemble, as it approaches new signal DK94 and Sapperton Short Tunnel. As on the previous page, the new signal is bagged over, awaiting commissioning at a later date. The short length of the tunnel can be clearly seen in this view, taken from a slightly different angle from the 1964 shot. A ramped vehicular access road has since been created down into the former 'quarry' area, which is now filled with plant and materials for the ongoing Swindon-Kemble redoubling project. *John Dagley-Morris/MJS*

SAPPERTON TUNNEL: Taken in the area between the two Sapperton tunnels, an unidentified 'Western' diesel-hydraulic emerges from the south portal of Sapperton Long Tunnel in the mid-1960s with 1A76, an up express for Paddington. Note the juxtaposition of the up distant signal for Sapperton Sidings signal box above the 'banner repeaters' (one obscured by the sighting board) showing the position of the splitting up home signals (seen opposite). The repeaters were almost certainly required due to sighting problems caused by Sapperton Short Tunnel. Similarly, it would have been very difficult, if not impossible, to position the up distant signal at the correct braking distance from the homes, which would have put it midway through the Long Tunnel. Your authors believe this to be an almost unique configuration of signals, even for the time, and would probably not be compliant with modern standards today. Due to the unusual configuration of tunnels and track layout, it is quite possible that the distant signal itself was repeated back in the Long Tunnel. *Garry Stroud collection*

We now find ourselves at the opposite (north) portal of Sapperton Long Tunnel (1 mile and 4 chains in length) as No 150261 emerges as 2Z33, the 1254 Kemble to Gloucester shuttle, on 19 August 2013. The train is passing one of the new up line signals, UK94R, which is effectively the 'distant' signal for UK94 at Sapperton, seen on page 77. The up line appears to have been relaid recently and the new location cabinets associated with the new signal can be seen to the right of the running lines. Cutting stabilisation work has also taken place recently, as evidenced by the gabion baskets and netting. *MJS*

SAPPERTON TUNNEL: 'WD' 2-8-0 No 90355 emerges from the north end of Sapperton Long Tunnel with a down goods service on an unrecorded date, presumably between June 1956 and November 1962, when she was shedded at Southall (81C), from where she was withdrawn. One assumes that her 34,125lb of tractive effort was sufficient to take her load unassisted up to the summit in Sapperton Tunnel. The positioning of the signals in this view is again of interest – the down distant signal for Frampton Crossing box is located on the up side of the line, presumably to obtain the best sighting for trains emerging from the tunnel. The 'banner repeater' next to the locomotive cab would have been for the same box's down home signal. Note the relatively good condition of the up direction 'Whistle' board.

This slightly more dramatic shot of the tunnel's north portal from milepost 96 was taken on the evening of Sunday 31 July 1977. Your authors hope that the intrepid photographer had already ensured that no up train was due behind him! Note the deteriorating condition of the 'Whistle' board. By this time all signalling associated with Frampton Crossing was long gone, and it would be another 36 years before we would see a fixed signal at this location again. *David Hopkins/Garry Stroud*

FRAMPTON CROSSING: On 14 September 1957 ex-GWR 'Castle' Class 4-6-0 No 5042 *Winchester Castle* approaches Frampton Crossing at speed down the 1 in 60 of Sapperton Bank with a Paddington to Cheltenham train. Note the neat and tidy lineside environment and the crossing keeper's cottage on the left. As at other locations on this line, the curvature has resulted in a signal being positioned on the opposite side of the line to which it applies, in order to provide drivers with the best possible sighting. *Mike Timms, Milepost 92½ collection*

Approaching Frampton Crossing from the north on 5 March 1961, 'Castle' Class 4-6-0 No 5051 *Earl Bathurst* would have been working hard to take the 3.55am Fishguard Harbour-Paddington service up the 1 in 60 bank to Sapperton Tunnel. This train would normally have run via the Severn Tunnel but was diverted via Gloucester and Kemble on this occasion. No 5051 was based in South Wales for whole of its BR life. Built in 1936 and named *Drysllwyn Castle*, it was renamed *Earl Bathurst* in August 1937, the name coming from a 'Dukedog' 4-4-0. After running more than 1,300,000 miles, she was withdrawn in May 1963 and sold for scrap. Fortunately she was saved for preservation and is now owned by the Great Western Society and based at Didcot, one of a total of eight 'Castle' Class locos preserved. *The late Richard Dagley-Morris, John Dagley-Morris collection*

FRAMPTON MANSELL: The enduring beauty of the 'Golden Valley' is epitomised in this view of No 37175 working towards Sapperton with a short ballast train, composed of just five 'Seacows', near Frampton Crossing on 15 May 1983.

On the same day No 50024 *Vanguard* heads the eight coaches of the 0805 Worcester (Shrub Hill) to Paddington express near Frampton Mansell. This well-travelled loco was built by English Electric at the Vulcan Foundry in Newton-le-Willows in 1967 and was finally withdrawn from service in 1991 after a bogie fire between Templecombe and Sherborne. The Class 50s have always been very popular with diesel enthusiasts, leading to no fewer than 18 of the 50 locomotives built now being preserved. *Both John Whitehouse*

Kemble to Stroud

CHALFORD: Running on well-maintained flat-bottom track, yet with the old telegraph poles still extant, No 47254 drops down from Frampton Crossing towards Chalford on Sunday 5 March 1978 with the diverted 1325 service from Paddington to Swansea. The locomotive appears to have recently been overhauled, as it is in immaculate BR 'corporate blue' livery. Spring has yet to put in an appearance in the Golden Valley, but the profusion of trees and other vegetation will no doubt continue to justify this name later in the year. *Garry Stroud*

On 1 July 2001 EWS-owned No 66090 stands at the rear of an engineer's train just to the south-east of Chalford. The brand new concrete sleepers on the adjacent track reveal the purpose of the possession, and old track panels can be seen stacked on the flat 'Salmon' wagons beyond the locomotive. It looks as if it could also soon be time to relay the jointed flat-bottomed track of the existing line, as evidenced by the new lengths of long welded rail in the 'six foot'. Perhaps the old track even dated from the era of the BTF film 'Making Tracks' in 1956? *MJS*

CHALFORD: Close to the location of the previous photograph, and on the same day, we see a gang of track renewals contractors at work near Chalford manually packing ballast and finishing work on the temporary clamped joints where the newly relaid track joins the older track. Notice the way that the rails are temporarily plated and clamped; the joints will probably be welded up during a follow-up possession, within a few days of the main works, with a Temporary Speed Restriction imposed during that time. To those of us used to the contemporary 'all orange' requirements for all track workers these days, the lack of orange 'high-vis' trousers on the part of most of these men seems almost quaint! *MJS*

No 66017 is on a ballast train just to the south of Chalford on 1 July 2001. Although 'Seacow' ballast wagons are still on the books of Network Rail at the time of writing, they are increasingly rarely used, so this view is all the more interesting as we see some of these older wagons in the process of being unloaded. Note the clouds of dust being raised as the train constantly moves forward at slow speed. *MJS*

CHALFORD: GWR steam railmotor No 2 sits in the down platform at Chalford in 1904, prior to working a local stopping service to Stonehouse. This was one of the very early, slab-fronted railmotors, which were not as attractive, in your author's opinion, as the later 'bow-ended' versions, one of which – No 93 – has been lovingly rebuilt and restored to operational condition by the Great Western Society at Didcot. The steam 'power bogie' of No 93 is a completely new build and was united with a wooden coach body that had been rebuilt in workshops on the Llangollen Railway.

Coupled with the opening of several new halts between Chalford and Stonehouse, the railmotor services had started on 12 October 1903 and became so popular that they quickly outgrew the limited accommodation available in a typical railmotor vehicle. Passenger loadings got so heavy that by 1905 the GWR was forced to provide a temporary road motor service between Chalford and Stroud to supplement the railmotors until more such trains became available. In some areas railmotors ran with auto-trailers, but this didn't work very well in the steeply graded Golden Valley, where such combinations found difficulty in keeping to time. The solution was eventually found to be the conversion of the railmotor vehicles to conventional auto-trailers, pulled or propelled by suitably fitted locomotives. *Lens of Sutton collection, MJS collection*

Just five months after working the final special excursions over the Tetbury and Cirencester Town branches, '14XX' 0-4-2 No 1472 is seen here at Chalford on the afternoon of 12 September 1964, having arrived with a train from Gloucester formed of two ex-GW coaches. The train will now draw out of station to set back into the down platform and form a return service to Gloucester. Chalford station was opened in August 1897, consisting of a neat brick-built main station building on the up platform, with a matching brick waiting room on the down side. There was no separate

footbridge – passengers used the road overbridge west of the station to cross from one platform to the other. The small goods yard on the up side also contained a siding and a shed to house the railmotors, a corrugated-iron structure on a timber framework that was even provided with an inspection pit; unfortunately the shed burned down on the night of 8 January 1919, together with railmotor No 48, which was stabled inside at the time. *John Dagley-Morris*

CHALFORD: Ex-GWR '54XX' 0-6-0PT No 5417 is seen arriving at Chalford with a train from Gloucester on 14 September 1957. Having initially been allocated to Southall, No 5417 was sent to Gloucester (Horton Road) (85B) in May 1951, remaining there until November 1959, when she spent three months at Neasden shed before moving on in February 1960 to Banbury, from where she was finally withdrawn in January 1961. Despite there being only 25 in the class, these useful little pannier tanks were seen in many corners of the former Great Western empire, but are especially associated with suburban workings in the London area. Being auto-fitted, No 5417 would have been gainfully employed on the Chalford auto-services, but while at Gloucester was also much used on the Cinderford branch trains in the Forest of Dean. The attractive station building is seen to good effect in this photograph, together with various other period details.

Incredible as it seems, this is the site of Chalford station on 27 September 2006. Greenery seems to have taken over, although the trees immediately adjacent to the up line mask the presence of a small, modern housing development, built on the site of the old goods yard. The overbridge carrying the A419 Stroud to Cirencester road can be seen in the background, although the former steps down to the platforms have long since disappeared. The down track looks in need of some weedkilling! *Mike Timms, Milepost 92½ collection/MJS*

The flora around railways is often home to some interesting wildlife, and the Chalford area is no exception. In this case, a Male Common Blue butterfly, *Polyommatus icarus*, was caught on camera by the line on 19 August 2013. *MJS*

Kemble to Stroud

CHALFORD: Towards the end of the Chalford local services, a number of non-auto-fitted locos were used. In this undated view, Hawksworth '94XX' pannier tank No 9453 is seen in the sylvan surroundings of the Golden Valley approaching Chalford's up distant signal with the 11.03am service from Gloucester. No 9453 was introduced into traffic in July 1951 and ended up being withdrawn from Gloucester (Horton Road) in November 1964, after being a servant of a variety of sheds and a wastefully short working life of only 13 years. *John Dagley-Morris*

ST MARY'S CROSSING: A little further west, we observe the approach to St Mary's Crossing from the Kemble direction on 16 May 1964. Despite appearances, this is no race between the '14XX' and the steam-hauled service in the background, for the auto-train on the down line is being propelled by No 1451 towards Stroud and Gloucester. Approaching on the up line is No 4954 *Plaish Hall* on a goods train for Swindon. Note how nature is 'bursting forth' as spring gets into its stride in this steeply sided valley. It is just possible to make out the footbridge at St Mary's Crossing Halt in the background, behind the goods train. *John Dagley-Morris*

ST MARY'S CROSSING: From an almost identical viewpoint to that seen in the bottom picture on the previous page, albeit it more than 45 years later, we are again treated to the sight of two steam locomotives, as No 4965 *Rood Ashton Hall* and No 5043 *Earl of Mount Edgcumbe* pass St Mary's Crossing signal box on 20 February 2010 with the southbound leg of 1Z43, 'The Great Western Incursion', a Tyseley-Didcot special charter. The trees may have grown somewhat in the intervening years, but many of the buildings are clearly the same, although the row of houses in the top-right hand corner appears to have received an extension at some point during that time. Both locomotives and the chocolate and cream stock are immaculate, a credit to their owners and operators, Vintage Trains of Tyseley Loco Works. *John Whitehouse*

Our photographic viewpoint edges ever closer to St Mary's Crossing as we observe BR Standard Class 4 4-6-0 No 75029 working an up goods train on 15 September 1960, assisted in the rear by 'Large Prairie' tank No 6137. The 'Standard 4' was delivered new from Swindon Works in 1954 and is fortunately now preserved many miles away from Gloucestershire, on the **North Yorkshire Moors Railway.** *The late Richard Dagley-Morris, John Dagley-Morris collection*

ST MARY'S CROSSING HALT: Another '94XX' pannier tank, No 9493, waits to restart its train from St Mary's Crossing Halt in September 1964, a mere two months before the Chalford services would be discontinued. The line came into being in 1845, but the halt was not opened until 12 October 1903, with the introduction of the GWR steam railmotor services between Stonehouse and Chalford, and was one of 20 halts or stations that used to exist between Swindon and Cheltenham. Closure came in November 1964 following the withdrawal of local stopping passenger services on the line. No trace of the halt remains today, but the signal box still exists to control the level crossing. *B. Mills collection, MJS collection*

ST MARY'S CROSSING HALT was located 98 miles 62 chains from London Paddington, and served industrial premises on the down side of the line from the main road, which are still in use today as offices, etc. A halt was opened here in 1903 when the Chalford to Stonehouse railmotor services started, the platforms being located immediately on the London side of the crossing, as seen here. The down platform was constructed of wood, while the up platform was a little more substantial, but passenger facilities on both were extremely basic. This is the view in 1959 looking towards Gloucester. The steel GWR footbridge was provided some time after the opening of the halt, following a fatality on the level crossing. The wooden 'constructions' located on either side of the down platform shelter were very unusual, and your authors know of nothing similar elsewhere. Modellers will no doubt note the graceful lamp standards attached to the footbridge and the unusual mounting for the station nameboard. There were once 16 stations or halts between Swindon Junction and Standish Junction, but now only Kemble, Stroud and Stonehouse remain open.

The present-day view on 27 September 2006 is of necessity slightly lower, due to the removal of the halt's platforms, revealing that the former station was constructed on a bridge! The removal of the footbridge reveals the retaining wall for the main road on the right. The attractive former signal box ceased to be a block post in 1970, when this area was resignalled under Gloucester Panel, but remains open as a manned level crossing box. *Roger Carpenter collection, MJS collection/MJS*

ST MARY'S CROSSING: This unusual view of the derelict footbridge was taken on 28 December 1978, looking down from the main road. Readers will note that the steps have been removed, and the rest of the structure would follow soon afterwards.

More than 33 years have passed since the previous photograph, and the former footbridge is now long gone, but St Mary's Crossing and signal box remain in daily use, as seen in this view taken on 20 June 2012. The level crossing gates have most creditably been renewed on a 'like for like' basis with 'heritage-style' replacements. With the road gates now open, the signals protecting the crossing will be maintained at danger, so it is safe for one of your authors to walk across and join the Mobile Operations Manager and Crossing Keeper (the latter can be seen standing inside the box) on 20 June 2012. The former crossing keeper's cottage still stands behind the signal box, now in private ownership. *Tim Venton/TM*

ST MARY'S CROSSING: This is the view looking north towards Stroud and Gloucester on what looks to be a rather damp and dismal winter's day, 28 December 1978. Both lines are now flat-bottomed track, although the up line nearest the camera appears still to be jointed, with fishplates every 60 feet.

An FGW HST in the earlier version of the blue livery approaches St Mary's Crossing at speed on 27 September 2006 forming an up express for Paddington. The approach road appears to have been recently resurfaced, as the crossing keeper and a resident from the adjacent cottage look on. Compared with the images from 1978, the main road above is 'doing its bit' in support of the proliferation of road warning signs of recent years. *Tim Venton/MJS*

Kemble to Stroud

ST MARY'S CROSSING: Taken from the safety of the signal box steps, South West Trains unit No 158890 approaches the crossing on Wednesday 20 June 2012 forming the 1154 service from Swindon to Cheltenham Spa. The unit has been leased to FGW to allow other 'Sprinter' sets to be deployed elsewhere and strengthen diagrams. Note the orange under-track crossings ('UTXs') under the front bogie of the unit, installed in recent years to protect cables that need to cross the formation. *MJS*

In this view looking south from the main road above the crossing on 28 December 1978, the partially dismantled footbridge can again be seen, together with the seemingly precarious location of the former halt platforms. The private owners of the crossing keeper's cottage seem to be doing a good job keeping the buildings in good condition. *Tim Venton*

BRIMSCOMBE: The 10.20am from Gloucester to Chalford departs from Brimscombe on 31 October 1964 behind pannier tank No 6412. Note the ongoing demolition of the stone locomotive shed in the background. No 6412 herself was later to be preserved by the Dart Valley Railway following withdrawal from British Railways service in November 1964. She was subsequently sold to the embryonic West Somerset Railway in early 1976, and made the journey from Devon under her own steam on British Rail metals. During her early life on the WSR she became something of a celebrity; not only did she work some of the first trains on the newly reopened line in 1976, but also became a star of the small screen that same summer when she masqueraded as 'The Flockton Flyer' in Southern Television's children's series of the same name. A second series was made during the summer of 1977, for which the WSR's second Bagnall 0-6-0ST *Vulcan* was specially restored to working order, so that she and No 6412 could 'race' for the cameras on the then double-track section between Bishops Lydeard and Norton Fitzwarren. Over the ensuing years, No 6412 became very closely identified with the WSR until the unthinkable happened. In 2009 the success of the WSR meant that larger locomotives were regularly required to haul the longer trains now required, and No 6412 was essentially 'surplus to requirements'. The wheel came full circle that year, when she was sold to the South Devon Railway and returned to her original preservation home at Buckfastleigh, where she is currently approaching the end of another overhaul. She was expected to return to service on the SDR during 2014. *John Dagley-Morris*

Kemble to Stroud

On 7 May 1964 an unidentified Churchward 2-8-0 approaches Brimscombe station with a down goods working. All railway infrastructure at Brimscombe appears to be intact in this view, although the A419 London Road is noticeably devoid of traffic. The train is approaching the down home signal for Brimscombe East box, which was slotted with the down distant for Brimscombe West on the same post; the latter signal is still at 'Caution', indicating that the section ahead is not yet clear for the '28XX' and her train. Brimscombe East box became plain 'Brimscombe' in 1964 when Brimscombe West box was closed. *John Stanford, Paul Stanford collection*

BRIMSCOMBE: No D1040 *Western Queen* is seen approaching Brimscombe station with a down express in an undated view that nonetheless post-dates the closure and demolition of the loco shed. The view is looking back up the bank towards St Mary's Crossing and Sapperton. The former GWR Type 7A Brimscombe East signal box, now just Brimscombe, dating from 1898 is prominent in this view; it closed in 1970 with the extension of signalling control to Gloucester Panel. *Mike Boakes collection*

BRIMSCOMBE: This delightful view looking east towards Swindon, taken on 12 June 1962, shows us just how much we have lost in railway architectural terms. The locomotive shed remains 'open for business' beyond the beautiful Brunellian 'chalet'-style station buildings. Brimscombe East signal box can just be glimpsed at the end of the up platform, just before the loco shed.

Yes, this is the same location, but virtually nothing remains on 27 September 2006, apart from the footpath crossing in the middle of the photograph, which marks the eastern end of the former platforms. A pair of modern signalling location cabinets stand sentinel next to the Down Kemble line, while above and to the left the (unseen) modern A419 road hums with levels of traffic that were scarcely conceivable at the time that the Beeching Report was being prepared in the early 1960s. *P. J. Garland, Roger Carpenter collection/MJS*

Kemble to Stroud

BRIMSCOMBE: This elevated view of the up station buildings at Brimscombe, taken on 12 June 1962 from the station footbridge, provides a wealth of architectural detail for the modeller. The historic building appears to still be in pretty good condition, yet within a few years it would be demolished by British Railways, an organisation that at the time appeared to be desperate to secure its share of the 'white heat of technology'. Note the wagons in the still-open goods yard, and the houses of the village on the hillside above the station. *P. J. Garland, Roger Carpenter collection*

This view of the former GWR loco shed at Brimscombe, taken circa 1960, is full of interesting period detail, including a safety handrail along the length of the shed to ensure that footplate staff didn't inadvertently get too close to the running lines. Opened in 1845, the then extended shed, surmounted by a new water tank, closed on 28 October 1963. 'Large Prairie' No 4111 (at the time allocated to Tyseley!) is stabled at the London end of the shed, no doubt awaiting its next banking turn up to Sapperton Sidings. Brimscombe East's up starting signal has been pulled off, together with the distant signal for Chalford, so it appears that a non-stop train is due. *Milepost 92½ collection*

BRIMSCOMBE BRIDGE HALT was 99 miles 74 chains from Paddington, and a mere 50 chains west of Brimscombe station itself. In this view dated 12 September 1964 we see Hawksworth '94XX' pannier tank No 9453 with the 11.20am stopper from Chalford to Gloucester approaching the halt. This loco was allocated new to Bristol (St Phillip's Marsh) in July 1951, moving to Gloucester (Horton Road) (85B) on 24 August 1964. She was withdrawn a mere three months later, just two months after this photograph was taken. The use of non-auto-fitted locos on the Chalford services became more common towards the end, necessitating a run-round at either end. *John Dagley-Morris*

A classic GWR/BR (WR) auto-train formation is seen at Brimscombe Bridge Halt on 16 May 1964, as No 1453 departs with the 3.10pm Gloucester-Chalford service. This halt had staggered platforms, the up platform being located beyond the road bridge in the background. This loco was another allocated to Horton Road at the time, specifically for the Chalford services, and was also withdrawn from there in November 1964. *John Dagley-Morris*

HAM MILL HALT was located at 100m 64ch, and was opened on 12 October 1903 to serve a number of nearby factories. On 24 October 1964 'Large Prairie' No 6113 slows to stop at the pre-cast concrete platforms of the halt with the 1.03pm train from Gloucester to Chalford. This was a much-travelled locomotive in BR days, with allocations ranging from the London area to Devon, the West Midlands and South Wales. She was withdrawn from Horton Road at the end of Western Region steam and scrapped in Cashmore's yard, Newport, in January 1966. Autumn is well into its stride in this view and the varying hues of the surrounding vegetation seem to justify the name 'Golden Valley'. There was a footpath crossing adjacent to the halt, which was fitted with bells warning of a train's approach, activated by trains passing over treadles on either side of the crossing. *John Dagley-Morris*

Seen earlier in this book languishing at Swindon after withdrawal, in this view the sun is still shining on a resplendent No 1011 *County of Chester* as she passes Ham Mill Halt, in the background, en route to Swindon on 20 September 1964 with the Stephenson Locomotive Society (Midland Area) train X83, the 'Farewell to the GWR County Class' special, which had departed from Birmingham Snow Hill at 9.50am and was diagrammed to run to Swindon and return. This fine locomotive was finally scrapped at Cashmore's yard, Newport, in March 1965. Note the mix of coaching stock in the train's formation, with a Hawksworth vehicle immediately behind the tender, followed by a Gresley example, then a BR Mark 1. *John Dagley-Morris*

BOWBRIDGE CROSSING HALT: The end is nigh for the local services on the Golden Valley line as No 1458 is seen near Bowbridge Crossing Halt with the 9.05am Stroud to Chalford roster on 31 October 1964, the last day of these services. The evidently chilly morning has given rise to a crisp exhaust from the locomotive, which was withdrawn from Horton Road shed within a month of these services finishing. *John Dagley-Morris*

No 1458 is seen again on the same day, departing from Bowbridge Crossing Halt amidst a cloud of exhaust steam with the 9.30am Chalford to Gloucester service. A solitary enthusiast, possibly a friend of the photographer, stands on the up platform to witness the spectacle. Within 24 hours any locals wishing to make the same journey would be thrown onto the mercy of the local bus companies. *John Dagley-Morris*

STROUD: This fine study of the exterior of Stroud's upside station buildings was taken on 28 December 1978. Posters of the era adorn the exterior of the building and a selection of period British-built cars can be seen parked outside. Just in case anyone turning up is unsure of the purposes of this building, a large 'British Rail' sign provides an unambiguous reminder of who is in charge here!

The present-day view was taken on 16 July 2014, and happily depicts a remarkably similar scene. The large 'British Rail' sign has gone, but the continued use of the 'corporate arrows' as the universal sign meaning 'the railway station is here' can be seen on the right. Thirty-five years of improvements in road traffic management have seen the introduction of a small roundabout, in the form of a colourful planter. Even the telephone box is still extant, but eagle-eyed readers will no doubt notice the additional storeys on the imposing red-brick building in the background. *Tim Venton/MJS*

Kemble to Stroud

STROUD: This splendid but undated view from the late 1950s shows the full panoply of steam-age infrastructure, as we see 'Castle' Class No 7000 *Viscount Portal* approaching with a Paddington-Gloucester express. A profusion of historical detail is on view for modellers, including the yard lamps built with old telegraph poles, a mass of GWR spear-top iron fencing and the 'GWR Stroud Station' painted on the goods shed wall. The large GWR Type 27C signal box, constructed in August 1905 to replace an earlier example, can be seen in the background. This was original called Stroud East, but became plain Stroud when the West signal box was closed in 1917. Goods traffic seems healthy, the goods yard here having been expanded in the 1880s, when a bank of soil was removed from the outside of the Imperial Hotel next to the station yard. Stroud is situated at the junction of a number of Cotswolds valleys and was central to the local woollen industry, so it was perhaps not surprising that goods traffic was buoyant for many years.

The present-day view on 3 September 2013 shows South West Trains-liveried unit No 158882 approaching with 2G83, the 1138 Swindon to Cheltenham Spa service operated by FGW. All evidence of sidings and the goods yard have now disappeared, although the fine stone goods shed remains, still emblazoned with the well-known painted legend painted on its walls. The signal box may also have gone, but we can see one of the new signals in the background, designated 'UK101R', this being the repeater ('distant') signal for the new UK101 signal. These are two of several new signals commissioned in August 2013 to split the previously long signal sections and provide more capacity on this line. *A. W. C. Mace, Milepost 92½ collection/MJS*

Stroud to Gloucester — Section 4

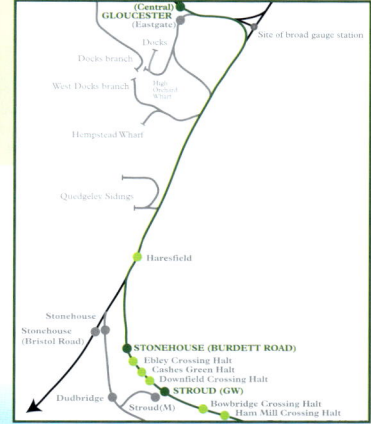

STROUD: On Wednesday 10 May 1978 the appropriately named photographer (!) captures Bristol-based DMU set B465 (comprising vehicles Nos W51307, W59474 and W51322 in a commendably clean BR overall 'corporate blue' livery) waiting at Stroud forming the 1110 Worcester (Shrub Hill) to Swindon service.

With the August 2013 blockade having been completed the previous day, an equally smart modern equivalent DMU – No 150106 – arrives at Stroud on Tuesday 3 September 2013 as 2B92, the 1119 Cheltenham Spa to Swindon local service.
Garry Stroud/MJS

BEARDS LANE CROSSING: On Wednesday 20 June 2012, and running over ex-GWR metals, SWT No 158890 operates the 1340 Cheltenham-Swindon local service past Beards Lane Crossing, west of Stroud. This pedestrian level crossing was located immediately behind the photographer and was very busy at certain times of day on account of a secondary school close to the railway. The interesting cloud formations hint at possible rain later!

As seen on 20 June 2012, the original crossing keeper's cottage at Beards Lane appears to have had one or two extensions built over the years. At the top of the tall (and rusty!) post, a small red box containing one of the audible crossing alarms can be seen. The signs provided on both sides for pedestrian users read 'Stop, Look, Listen. Do not cross when warning sounds. Beware – Trains arrive soon after alarm sounds'. Beards Lane was formerly a road crossing and had been provided with a small signal box, which was removed when the crossing was downgraded to pedestrian use only and the audible alarms provided.

The posts carrying the old alarms are still extant in the third view, dated 16 July 2014, but the crossing is now closed and new 'palisade' fences block the former pedestrian accesses. The reason for this is quite clear: the large green footbridge in the background was opened in October 2013 to replace both this and the adjacent Downfield Crossing, a mere 200 yards or so to the west of Beards Lane. *MJS (2)/TM*

Stroud to Gloucester

DOWNFIELD CROSSING HALT was located at 102m 69ch and adjacent to the foot crossing of the same name. It was opened on 12 October 1903 and in this view plays host to No 6412 and its up local train on an unrecorded date in 1964. Underneath the grime, the loco is in lined green livery. The area around this and other halts in the Stroud area was not entirely rural even then, and is even more built up now, being essentially part of the greater Stroud urban area, if that's not too grandiose a description for this pleasant Cotswolds district. Modellers will note the traditional ex-GWR 'pagoda' waiting shelter partially visible on the down platform.

With approximately 18 months of life remaining for Downfield Crossing Halt, 'Modified Hall' No 6993 *Arthog Hall* passes with an up express in May 1963; the foot crossing can be seen between the tender and first coach. No trace remains of the platforms today, and even the foot crossing has been closed and replaced by the nearby footbridge at Beards Lane. *Keith Jones collection/Cassandra Murdoch collection, MJS* collection

Stroud to Gloucester

CASHES GREEN HALT was a mere 34 chains to the west of Downfield Crossing and served a continuation of the same residential area of the Stroud suburbs. On 18 March 1962 'Castle' Class 4-6-0 No 5084 *Reading Abbey* is seen passing through with F21, the 9.55am Paddington to Swansea express, which has been diverted via Stroud and Gloucester due to scheduled maintenance work in the Severn Tunnel. The loco was shedded at 81A (Old Oak Common) all her life and was withdrawn on 14 July 1962. Note the very tall telegraph poles, presumably to provide sufficient clearance over the brick road overbridge.

A very youthful trainspotter totters in a seemingly precarious fashion at the top of the down platform ramp at Cashes Green Halt on 23 January 1965, although a grown-up, possibly the photographer, is no doubt on hand to prevent any accidental loss of balance! Where is he now, one wonders! The halt, opened on 21 January 1930 following requests from local residents, had been closed for more than two months at the time this photo was taken. The wooden construction of the platforms of this relatively late addition to the inventory of local stations can be clearly seen, and the concrete posts for the oil lamps will be of interest to modellers, as will the arrangement of stay wires for the tall telegraph poles. *The late Richard Dagley-Morris, John Dagley-Morris collection/Keith Jones collection*

EBLEY CROSSING HALT: On 5 March 1961 'Castle' Class No 7000 *Viscount Portal* is seen passing Ebley Crossing Halt (103m 52ch) with the 11.55am Swindon-Cheltenham Spa local service. The loco was allocated to Gloucester (Horton Road) (85B) at that time, but was subsequently transferred to Worcester (85A) prior to withdrawal on 28 December 1963. The overall feel of the surrounding area is now more rural, and this was the last of the halts in the Stroud urban area. The next station for this train will be Stonehouse (Burdett Road). *John Dagley-Morris*

STONEHOUSE: With Stonehouse (Burdett Road) station in the background, No 1445 accelerates away with its load of two Hawksworth auto-coaches forming the 11.20am Gloucester to Chalford local on 16 May 1963. Note the old concrete 'pot' sleepers beneath the seemingly moribund down refuge siding to the left of the train. *John Dagley-Morris*

Wreathed in steam, No 1458 looks to be in commendably clean condition as she approaches Stonehouse on 31 October 1964 with the 09.30am Chalford to Gloucester local. The loco is propelling her load of two auto-coaches; the lamp under the chimney is actually the train's tail lamp. The lattice footbridge in the background looks to be the location from which the previous photograph was taken. *John Dagley-Morris*

Stroud to Gloucester

STONEHOUSE: On 18 March 1962 No 6941 *Fillongley Hall* approaches Stonehouse station with 1H58, the 1.20pm Paddington to Cheltenham Spa express. From June 1956 to May 1964 this loco was allocated to sheds in Devon and South Wales, so it is strange that it should be working this train. Perhaps it had worked to Paddington on an unplanned basis and was being returned to its home shed. It would end its days at Pontypool Road (86G) in May 1964. The short up loop and sidings seem overgrown and disused, but a couple of 16-ton mineral wagons and a vacuum-braked five-plank open wagon demonstrate that the goods yard on the down side is still active. There was in fact considerable goods traffic prior to closure of the goods yard in 1964, especially coal. At one time both Standish Hospital and Gloucestershire County Council had coal delivered to the GW station at Stonehouse – that for the County Council was intended for use in its fleet of steam roadrollers! There was also a brick and tile works adjacent to the London end of the station, which also received coal inwards and despatched bricks and tiles outwards.

This is the same view from the station footbridge looking towards the south-east on 3 September 2013. The elegant stone goods shed has gone, as has all other evidence of the goods yard and other sidings. The houses seen in the background of the 1962 view are still present, and new housing has appeared on the up side of the line as well. A huge evergreen tree obscures much of the present-day view! *The late Richard Dagley-Morris, John Dagley-Morris collection/MJS*

STONEHOUSE: Further steam-age infrastructure is evident in this delightful view of Stonehouse on 12 June 1962. Note the differing levels of the down platform, which was eventually rebuilt to a consistent, standard height in 1976. The station became known as 'Burdett Road' in 1951, to avoid confusion with the nearby ex-Midland station on the Bristol-Gloucester main line, known as 'Bristol Road'. The GWR Type 8A signal box dating from 1922 can be seen just beyond the 1890 station footbridge.

With HST power car No 43149 on the rear, 1L50, the 1031 Cheltenham Spa to London Paddington service, restarts from the Stonehouse stop on Tuesday 3 September 2013. The current platforms are roughly half the length of the originals seen in the 1962 photograph, with the result that only the first two coaches of HSTs can be platformed here. This is made possible by the use of selective door opening fitted to all FGW HST sets, enabling doors not platformed to remain locked. On-train announcements direct passengers to the correct coaches from which to alight. *P. J. Garland, Roger Carpenter collection/MJS*

STONEHOUSE: No 1449 pauses at Stonehouse in June 1963 on a Gloucester to Chalford local train. Modellers may wish to note the underside details of the two canopies, including what appear to be cast support brackets. The stone station buildings are essentially as originally built when the station opened.

With the booked timetable restored following the August 2013 redoubling blockade, No 150106 draws into Stonehouse station on Tuesday 3 September 2013 with 2B92, the 1119 Cheltenham Spa to Swindon stopper. Eagle-eyed readers won't fail to notice that the appealing old stone station buildings are no longer extant. Back in the early 1970s British Rail aspired to close the station, partly on the grounds that the buildings were no longer safe and needed to be demolished. Local efforts to save the station resulted in the original stone buildings being listed, yet this eventually caused BR to announce the closure of the station on the grounds that the listing meant that a more comprehensive and thus costly renovation would be required, which BR felt it could not afford. The Department of the Environment (which had responsibility for transport at the time) eventually agreed to remove the listed status and permit the demolition of both station buildings, which would be rebuilt in stone, but in a much simpler style. The up platform shelter seen in this view thus dates from 1977, whereas its down platform equivalent itself required demolition in recent years, although there are plans to provide a new building.

Keith Jones collection/MJS

STONEHOUSE: A mere 12 years prior to acquiring celebrity status on the West Somerset Railway, auto-fitted pannier tank No 6412 waits at Stonehouse on 26 October 1964 with a Gloucester to Chalford local. At least two fare-paying passengers have alighted! Note the tight geometry of the crossover between the platforms.

The comparative modern-day view sees power car No 43093 leading 1L58, the 1220 Cheltenham Spa to Paddington service, as it prepares to stop at Stonehouse station on Wednesday 2 July 2014. The iron railings appear to be the original GWR pattern, and the 1977 stone shelter can just be seen behind the smart power car. Modern vandal-proof metal seats now adorn both platforms, while the site of the 1977 down platform structure is out of view to the left. Significant tree growth has taken place in the intervening 50 years, but the row of brick houses visible in the 1962 view is still there today. *Mike Boakes collection/MJS*

Stroud to Gloucester

STONEHOUSE: A slightly grubby No 6852 *Headbourne Grange* is seen here on 18 March 1962 approaching Stonehouse with the 8.50am Cheltenham-Paddington express. The station at Burdett Road is nearby, as seen from the presence of the up refuge siding adjacent to the train. Although allocated to Bristol (St Phillip's Marsh) (82B) shed when photographed, it had nominally been transferred to Newport (Ebbw Junction) by this date but, with the shed plate missing here, it had presumably not yet made it to South Wales. *The late Richard Dagley-Morris, John Dagley-Morris collection*

On 18 March 1962 we find ourselves just to the north of Stonehouse Burdett Road, as a commendably clean No 5016 *Montgomery Castle* gets into its stride on GW metals proper, having just left behind Standish Junction and the metals of the parallel GW and Midland lines. The train is 1A10, the 3.55pm Fishguard Harbour-Paddington express, which has been diverted via Awre, Gloucester and the Golden Valley line due to maintenance works in the Severn Tunnel. Sadly, this paragon of steam motive power cleanliness would be withdrawn a mere six months later. *The late Richard Dagley-Morris, John Dagley-Morris collection*

STANDISH JUNCTION: Immediately to the south of the actual junction at Standish is a high overbridge carrying a local farm track, from which our photographer has obtained this fine view of No 50044 *Exeter* on Thursday 5 November 1981, working the 1023 Manchester (Piccadilly) to Plymouth 'cross-country' express, which has already taken the down Charfield line at the junction on its way towards the South West. The two tracks at the higher level on the right are the Golden Valley line to Stroud and Swindon. The loco has since been preserved on the Severn Valley Railway.

Almost 32 years later the scene is to all intents and purposes unchanged, although the rolling stock has moved on a generation. Climbing the 1 in 347 gradient away from Standish Junction, No 150104 heads towards its next stop at Stonehouse with 2B92, the 1119 Cheltenham Spa to Swindon local service, on Thursday 17 October 2013. Modellers will note the metal ladder linking the upper and lower levels, to avoid PW staff having to walk 'the long way round'. Note also the earth-moving plant on the embankment in the distance, which was being used during overnight and weekend possession to stabilise that section of bank. *Garry Stroud/MJS*

STANDISH JUNCTION: Our photographer has stationed himself at the physical junction at Standish, just to the south of the wooden Midland Railway signal box, as No 7024 *Powis Castle* passes on 5 March 1961 with A87, the 11.20am Carmarthen-Paddington express, another service diverted due to maintenance works in the Severn Tunnel. This member of the 'Castle' Class never saw Great Western livery, being delivered new to the Western Region of British Railways in July 1949. It spent its whole life allocated to Old Oak Common and Oxley (Wolverhampton), from where it was withdrawn in September 1963 after less than 14 years of revenue-earning service.

Although the signal box has long since been superseded and removed and the junction pointwork rearranged, the location is still recognisably the same as the 1961 view, although the old iron road bridge has also been completely rebuilt in concrete and brick during the intervening period. Unlike the 1961 view, 1G38, the 1336 Paddington to Cheltenham express seen here on 17 October 2013, is a northbound service, which is approaching the junction from the Kemble direction. The railway here still gives the appearance of a four-track main line, but this is deceptive because we are really seeing the confluence of two double-track lines, which merge just north of the road bridge to become a double track railway northwards to Gloucester. *John Dagley-Morris/MJS*

HARESFIELD: Under a glowering winter sky, No D156 approaches Haresfield level crossing on Monday 7 January 1974 with a southbound inter-regional working towards Bristol and the South West. The level crossing has already been reduced to pedestrian status only, although the former signal box still survives, albeit painted a slightly unexpected shade of green! The railway used to consist of four tracks at this location, which formerly continued northwards as far as Tuffley Junction, where the up and down Midland tracks split from the double line of the GWR as they headed towards their respective stations in Gloucester. Haresfield was unusual in that the station platforms were only provided on the two Midland tracks, on the left-hand side of the formation as we see it here; they were located immediately beyond the level crossing and signal box. No platforms were provided on the GWR side.

On 16 July 2014 the weather was considerably warmer than in the 1974 shot, as an unidentified five-car CrossCountry 'Super Voyager' set passes Haresfield forming 1V58, the 0900 Glasgow Central to Penzance service. The surrounding vegetation and the Beacon Hotel rooftop help identify the location, as if the sign in the foreground wasn't sufficient! The 'Super Voyager' is about to pass over the pedestrian crossing, which is now controlled with red and green warning lights for the safety of users. Although the running lines here were reduced from four tracks to two when Gloucester Panel was commissioned in the late 1960s, up and down goods loops were also provided, the up loop being visible beyond the crossing. These remain in regular use to this day, being used to recess and regulate the passage of freight services.
Garry Stroud/MJS

Stroud to Gloucester

HARESFIELD: Approaching Haresfield crossing from the south on 7 July 1962, on the ex-GWR lines, is No 5000 *Launceston Castle* with the 1.45pm Paddington to Cheltenham Spa express, which had departed from Swindon at 3.34pm. The locomotive looks to be in somewhat tatty condition, although it would nonetheless not have been taxed by its five-coach load. It was withdrawn from Oxley shed on 22 November 1964.

Some 52 years later another 'Super Voyager', No 221134, approaches Haresfield from the south with 1S53, the 1325 Plymouth to Edinburgh CrossCountry service, on Wednesday 16 July 2014. The down goods loop begins immediately to the south of the pedestrian crossing. *John Dagley-Morris/MJS*

HARESFIELD: Unmistakably on the former GWR side at Haresfield on 7 July 1962, No 7017 *G. J. Churchward* passes the former Midland station on the left with the 4.00pm Cheltenham Spa to Paddington express. This loco was delivered new to Cardiff (Canton) shed in August 1950 and was withdrawn from Old Oak Common (81A) in February 1963, after a working life of only just over 12 years.

On 17 October 2013 No 66956 in Freightliner HeavyHaul livery speeds the delayed 0852 Rugeley 'B' Power Station to Stoke Gifford coal empties past Haresfield. This train was running 46 minutes late on that date, due to having been delayed by an incident on another freight near Gloucester, to which the fire brigade had to be called as a precaution (although nothing serious transpired!). *The late Richard Dagley-Morris, John Dagley-Morris collection/MJS*

Stroud to Gloucester

TUFFLEY JUNCTION: Approaching Tuffley Junction, with the ex-Midland lines to the left, auto-fitted pannier tank No 6437 passes with the 1240 Gloucester to Stroud local in September 1960, shortly after the loco had transferred to Gloucester from Severn Tunnel Junction. This loco was withdrawn in July 1963, although three examples of the class now survive in preservation.

On a disappointingly dull period during the afternoon on Thursday 17 October 2013, No 66142 heads south from Gloucester, and is approaching the present-day Tuffley crossovers with 6V92, a Corby to Margam empty steel working. This was diverted on this occasion, via Yate, due to the derailment of the Tesco train at Gloucester station earlier in the week. Note how the lineside vegetation has grown up in the intervening years. *John Dagley-Morris/MJS*

GLOUCESTER SOUTH JUNCTION: No 4090 *Dorchester Castle* passes the junction on 19 February 1961 with A53, the 10.45am 'Q' service from Cardiff to Paddington, which was booked to run when the 6.45am from Fishguard Harbour was running late. Gloucester South Junction signal box, with its reinforced wartime brick base, can be seen in the distance, as ex-LMS 4F No 43985 waits on the down goods line next to the yard. *Dorchester Castle* was withdrawn from Cardiff East Dock shed in June 1963, having previously been a much-travelled loco on many parts of the former GWR system. *John Dagley-Morris*

No 7813 *Freshford Manor* is seen on former Midland metals between Engine Shed Junction and Gloucester South Junction on 7 October 1962 with the 12.35pm Cheltenham to Swindon train, which on that date was diverted away from Gloucester without stopping or reversing, due to engineering work at Tramway Junction in Gloucester itself. Despite having been another widely travelled loco, *Freshford Manor* would not become one of the nine 'Manors' out of 30 to be preserved; it was withdrawn from Horton Road shed in May 1965 and scrapped at Bird's yard in Swansea. *The late Richard Dagley-Morris, John Dagley-Morris collection*

Stroud to Gloucester

TRAMWAY JUNCTION was to the east of the two Gloucester stations, and on 20 June 1959 BR Standard 9F 2-10-0 No 92238 trundles over what would become known as Horton Road level crossing in later years with a goods for the Swindon line. The loco was delivered new in September 1958 but only lasted in service for a mere seven years, being withdrawn from Severn Tunnel Junction in November 1965 and scrapped at Cashmore's yard in Newport shortly thereafter. The tracks in the immediate foreground crossing underneath the 9F lead to Engine Shed Junction and the line towards Cheltenham.

On 11 July 2007 two-car unit No 158766, still in ex-Trans Pennine livery but now working as part of the FGW fleet, leaves Gloucester with a service to Taunton. The level crossing barriers belong to Horton Road level crossing, which is directly controlled from Gloucester Panel signal box, situated immediately to the right, albeit out of view. *The late Richard Dagley-Morris, John Dagley-Morris collection/MJS*

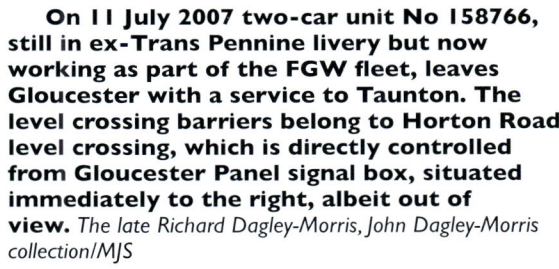

GLOUCESTER: We now approach the city of Gloucester on Thursday 20 June 1985, to see power car No 43028 leading the 1302 Cheltenham Spa to Paddington InterCity express away from Central station and around the curve towards Gloucester Yard Junction (formerly Gloucester South Junction). Horton Road level crossing is just out of view to the left of the train. The area next to the railway in the foreground and to the left has been redeveloped in recent years. *Garry Stroud*

Following the resignalling of the area in 1968, and the eventual closure of the Tuffley Loop and Gloucester Eastgate in 1975, what was formerly the GWR station at Gloucester Central was much rebuilt, and a very long platform extension was provided across the formation of the former lines to Eastgate station. This is now one of the longest public passenger platforms in the UK, although it is split into two separate platforms for operational purposes by a crossover and associated signalling. On Tuesday 1 June 1982 No 31304 was summoned from Horton Road stabling point to haul a DMU set consisting of vehicles Nos W51384, W59492, W51339, which had evidently suffered some kind of mechanical problem. This ensemble would continue towards Cheltenham as the 1405 Swindon to Cheltenham local service, albeit now running some 25 minutes late. The raw earth of the recently developed formation from Eastgate station can be seen in the foreground. *Garry Stroud*

Stroud to Gloucester

GLOUCESTER: With the Gloucester and District Irish Society occupying the large brick building in the background, we see a variety of first-generation BR diesels at Gloucester (Horton Road) depot on Tuesday 11 October 1983 – visible are Nos 20187, 20179, 46033 and 37247. The former GWR steam locomotive depot had largely been demolished by this time, as evidenced by the open space adjacent to the running lines, but was still staffed and used for stabling and light maintenance.

Before even these sidings were subsequently clipped out of use, we can see No 47200 *The Fosse Way* and No 47033 *The Royal Logistic Corps*, together with a former GUV (General Utility Van) parcels van, stabled on the remains of Horton Road shed on 11 July 2007. All rolling stock in this picture then belonged to the Gloucester-based Cotswold Rail, although the company would later cease trading and its assets sold on to other train operators. *Garry Stroud/MJS*

GLOUCESTER: After having worked the 0815 Plymouth to Leeds cross-country service into Gloucester Central on Saturday 27 December 1980, No 46031 leaves the station for Horton Road stabling point. The same loco would later return towards the South West with the 0920 Liverpool to Penzance service, which departed from Gloucester at 1216. The closure of Eastgate station had removed a very useful facility for cross-country services and the length of time it took to reverse and run round a loco-hauled train would subsequently result in almost all such trains ceasing to call at Gloucester. Most of today's services operated by the train operator CrossCountry Trains no longer call here, although good connections are generally available via Cheltenham Spa. Note the five stabling sidings to the right of the picture, three of which remain in use to this day.

A few years earlier, and further along Platform 1, we see the station on 7 November 1977, with a ballast train of 'Seacow' hopper wagons occupying one of the through lines. Parcels vans occupy the stabling sidings to the right. *Garry Stroud/Dennis Weaver, MJS collection*

Stroud to Gloucester

GLOUCESTER: On 19 February 1961 No 4090 *Dorchester Castle* is seen departing from Gloucester Central with A53, the 10.45am 'Q' express from Cardiff to Paddington, which was again diverted via Gloucester. No 7926 *Willey Hall* is backing onto the 12.35pm Cheltenham to Swindon local in the adjacent platform road. The board crossing in the foreground is located in approximately the same position as the current station footbridge.

On 11 April 2013 No 43092 waits to leave with 1L50, the 1031 Cheltenham Spa to London Paddington service. The combination of Platforms 1 and 2 at Gloucester now forms one of the longest platforms in the country. The two centre roads are happily still with us and much used by the frequent freight services between South Wales and the North. Platform 4 on the right-hand side is mostly used by northbound services between Maesteg and Cheltenham (Arriva Trains Wales) and between Cardiff and Nottingham (CrossCountry). Note the new footbridge with lifts. *The late Richard Dagley-Morris, John Dagley-Morris collection/MJS*

GLOUCESTER: In this undated view we see an unusual pairing of BR Standard Class 5 4-6-0 No 73002 with 'Jubilee' No 45683 *Hogue* at Gloucester Central on a Cardiff to Newcastle service. Note the large water tower in the background. What appears to be a DMU waits in the up bay behind the leading loco.

Stroud to Gloucester

The 'GW150' celebrations in 1985 saw a multitude of steam-hauled specials across the former GWR system, willingly put on by the Western Region. Here at Gloucester Central on 26 August 1985 we join the crowds of well-wishers to see **No 6000** *King George V* on one such working, with a smart rake of chocolate and cream Mark 1 coaches in tow. The former up bay platform is now disused. *David Hopkins/Dennis Weaver, MJS collection*

GLOUCESTER: On 30 April 1962 No 1409 departs from the old Gloucester Central with the 7.55am stopper to Chalford. This loco was a sporadic but long-time servant of 85B, and ended its career at Gloucester (Barnwood) (85C) on 2 November 1963. It is approximately in the position of the modern footbridge at the current station, but what is prominent in this view is the old covered footbridge between Central and Eastgate stations. A maroon Gresley panelled coach and an ex-LMS van are stabled in the carriage sidings to the left. *The late Richard Dagley-Morris, John Dagley-Morris collection*

BOWBRIDGE CROSSING HALT: On a gloriously sunny 12 September 1964, No 1458 is seen close to Bowbridge Crossing Halt, operating as the 12.30 p.m. Chalford-Gloucester shuttle. Officially the loco had been withdrawn three months earlier, so, perhaps, as the smokebox is devoid of shed plate, it has been brought out of store for a short period. *John Dagley-Morris*